12.95

BETWEEN CHAOS AND NEW CREATION

Theology & Life

THEOLOGY AND LIFE SERIES

Other Titles in Preparation

Theology and Life Series   19

Between Chaos and New Creation
Doing Theology at the Fringe

by

Enda McDonagh

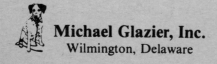
Michael Glazier, Inc.
Wilmington, Delaware

Published in 1986 by Michael Glazier, Inc., 1935 West Fourth
Street, Wilmington, Delaware 19805 by arrangement with Gill
and Macmillan, Ltd, Goldenbridge, Inchicore, Dublin 8.
©Copyright 1986 by Enda McDonagh. All rights reserved.
Library of Congress Catalog Card Number: 86-72360.
International Standard Book Number: 0-89453-615-X. Printed
in Great Britain.

for Bekan

Contents

Sources

Gospel and Culture (based on address to Pax Romana International Conference, *Gospel and Culture in Europe at the End of the Twentieth Century*, Innsbruck, September 1985)

The Grace of Unbelief (*The Furrow*, 1983)

Set Free for Freedom (*The Furrow*, 1984)

Peace-Makers or Justice Seekers? (presented to the Human Rights Commission, Pax Christi International, Vicenza, May 1986)

Creative Reconciliation (based on papers to conference on *'Politics and Forgiveness'* Oxford, July 1985 and to the International Council of Christians and Jews, Dublin, 1985)

The Challenge of the Holocaust (Cardinal Bee Memorial Lecture to the International Council of Christians and Jews, London, March 1986)

Sacraments and Society (*Being and Truth, Festschrift for Professor John Macquarrie*, 1986)

Irish Contexts and Theological Methods (published in *Challenges to Theology*, 1986)

Dying for the Cause (*Concilium*, 1983)

Northern Ireland (partly published in *The Furrow*, November 1984 and June 1985)

The Christian in Politics (in *Ireland in the Contemporary World*, ed. James Dooge, Gill and Macmillan 1986)

Artisans of a New Creation (based on articles in *The Furrow*, November 1978 and November 1985)

Free to Hope (in *Freedom to Hope?* ed. Falconer, McDonagh, MacReamoinn, Columba Press 1985)

1.

Introduction

Real and Present Dangers

'Apocalypse Now' has a familiar and fundamentalist ring. The ring is bound to become more familiar and, no doubt, more fundamentalist over the next fourteen years. The signs are abundant with the four horsemen at full gallop. The mushroom cloud which overshadows all other signs for so many has for backing, as the language of pop might put it, acts and threats of local war, of terrorist attack and counter-attack. The prospect of total annihilation in nuclear war, as climax to currents, threats and actions, is regularly obscured by the prospect of regional annihilation through famine and disease. And these are only the large-scale indicators that frighten even the comfortable and secure as they look up from the present soothing distractions to face the disturbing present realities and future prospects.

There is even less reassurance to be derived from the recent past. A century which has known two world wars, the Nazi Holocaust of the Jews, the Stalinist purges and a hundred lesser destructive tyrannies and massacres, may be brought happily to an end — provided it is not the end feared by so many alert and sensible people. The 'Apocalypse Now' syndrome is no longer the preserve of religious fundamentalists or political crazies, although they may well contribute to its realisation. The sane and serious have to take note of the technical capacity now available to the human race and of the record of political and moral incapacity displayed by its political leadership in the use of that technology. Pacification by obliteration and famine in the shadow of meat and grain

1

mountains offer adequate comment on the continuous disastrous combination of technical achievement with moral and political failure.

In such a context faith appears increasingly futile. Theology, faith-reflexion, appears an absurd enterprise, at best a form of religious and intellectual tranquilliser, at worst a deceitful distraction of people from the dignified protests and modest practical moves which might be made against accelerating insanity.

Yet many people read the world text quite differently. Despite Chernobyl and Challenger, even despite Hiroshima, Auschwitz and Gulag, technological and human progress are seen as contemporary, desirable and possible. It is a more difficult reading to defend than it was at the end of the nineteenth century or even fifty years ago. To very many people it is still unquestionably the correct reading. To many others, despite serious reservations, it seems the only possible one if the human race is to go on. It must go on. It will go on. Without sharing the taste for heroic absurdity of a Camus character or a Beckett tramp, so many human beings resonate with the final words in that Beckett trilogy, 'I'll go on'. 'Apocalypse 2000' can and must be avoided. The will to survive will prevail. So much these people's gut instinct tells them, and, in more optimistic mood, that progress is still possible.

There is not much room for faith or faith-reflexion in this more optimistic scenario either. It is a secular hope and a secular struggle. Religion may even be a complicating and threatening factor, as the rise of Islamic fundamentalism in particular portends. For the secular hopefuls the religious record in this century is no more encouraging than the political record is for the pessimists.

There remain the escapists. 'Let them destroy one another. We won't fight.' But where to escape? One might seek age-old escapes, and many do, in alcohol, drugs, sex, the dizzy dance of pleasure, only to find it becoming increasingly macabre under Hiroshima or even Chernobyl clouds. A territory seems more attractive and plausible. An island perhaps, neutral, non-aligned, nuclear-free . . . the island of the rainbow, where time goes on a holiday, as the romantic German travel-books used to say. What other island than the Island of Saints and Scholars, Ireland. It can't work of course. Radioactive clouds and nuclear winters do not respect neutrality or insularity.

The other problems of the modern world are also evident in Ireland. Political violence in Northern Ireland, family breakdown, unemployment, violent crime, drug abuse form the daily substance of Irish news bulletins. They may be all the more painful for being so new, at least on their present scale. There is no escape from the current crisis in Ireland.

Ireland's fringe existence affects the timing and the type of the contemporary crisis as experienced there. It will also affect how Ireland responds to the crisis. As Christian faith and Church, dominantly but not exclusively in the Catholic tradition, have been integral for so long to Irish society, the crisis has enormous implications for both. Much attention has been devoted to the effects of the crisis on family as the recent constitutional referenda on abortion and divorce indicate. The vigorous debate and division which emerged were between Christians and, for demographic reasons, mainly between Catholics. Many other debates and divisions on Northern Ireland, Central America, neutrality, unemployment, economic and educational policy have revealed profound stresses in Irish society about how it should relate to the wider contemporary world and how it should define its own identity and resources. Faith and Church have to share these stresses or otherwise retire into irrelevance. In sharing the stresses and struggling to respond, Irish faith and Church can benefit from theological and pastoral responses already developed elsewhere. Irish faith and Church must also develop their own distinctive timing and type of response, which will, if valid, make a contribution to response in a wider world.

This book is basically a collection of articles and papers prepared over the last few years in the context of a world in crisis and of an Ireland sharing that crisis but in its own fashion. They have been revised and completely recast in some cases. About half are published here for the first time.

Irish theology, as part of universal theology, and yet distinctive in facing Irish challenges and seeking to deploy Irish resources, has been developing its own momentum over the last decades. This volume is an attempt to contribute to that development but in interaction with universal or catholic theology. The two sections of the book, Confronting the Modern World and Constructing a Local Theology, underline the distinction but maintain the interaction in individual chapters in each section.

The choice between chaos and new creation, as key to theological understanding of and response to the contemporary situation, requires further explanation and justification. Their recurrence in differing forms in handling individual issues gradually led to their identification as critical categories of analysis, but are they theological categories? New Testament usage based on Old Testament background gives theological respectability to 'new creation'. 'Chaos' is more elusive in meaning, usage and origin, although it might easily invoke as basis the pre-creation or the post-fall states described in Genesis. Neither expression has received much recent theological discussion, although they are sometimes recognised as powerful theological symbols or metaphors.

The vogue for 'metaphorical theology' in recent writing has rightly emphasised the necessarily metaphorical or symbolic character of all theological discourse. This does not undermine or impoverish the significance of theological statements. It does draw attention to their limitations and to their enormous possibilities. Without metaphorical, symbolic and analogical language — I take all three to belong to the same family — God-talk would be simply impossible. The truth-possibilities of such language may not match the divine reality but they greatly exceed the truth-possibilities of any attempts at narrowly literal and conceptual language about God. In chapter 9 on method, these problems are given fuller consideration. Here it is important to underline the symbolic, poetic character of 'chaos' and 'new creation', and their consequent rich truth-possibilities.

Chaos and creation, fresh chaos and new creation, convey much of the rhythm or dialectic of the Hebrew scriptures. The early chapters of Genesis provide powerful examples of this. The original chaos is gradually (over six days) transformed by the creative Spirit of God, and this transformation reaches its climax in the creation of human beings. In these poetic accounts of origins, chaos is both void or nothingness and formlessness or primitive form, subjected to the creating and transforming activity of God. Through chapters one to three of Genesis, progressive transformation proceeds to the point of community between God and his created images, human beings, now charged with the care and development of the created cosmos, and so given the dignity of co-creators.

Humanity's promethean reach for equality with God in chapter three precipitates fresh chaos, the distortion and destruction of the forms of harmony and mutual enrichment which had united God, humanity and cosmos. This deformation entered deeply into the fabric of the created world. Fratricide of Abel by Cain (Gen. 4) and the breakdown of human communication in the Tower of Babel story (Gen. 11) reveal the range and depth of the chaotic deformation. The continuing commitment (promise and covenant) provided for successive re-formations and re-creations in the stories of Noah, Abraham, Moses, David and the other heroes and covenants of Israel. All this was response to Israel's continuing relapse into chaos in the pursuit of false gods and self-destruction.

The apparently unbreakable sequence of new divine creation and fresh human chaos reached what proved a paradoxical climax in Jesus. The paradox had been anticipated in (Deutero-) Isaiah's vision of the 'suffering servant' (chapter 53). Entry into and surrender to the very disintegration and destruction caused by human beings themselves (truly human chaos) became the key to overcoming the chaos and finally breaking the sequence. New creation in its definitive form emerged from the surrender of the Creator-God to the destructive, anti-creation, chaotic forces of humanity. Humanly induced chaos became the gateway to divinely restored creation.

New Creation and Chaos after Jesus

God's definitive achievement in Jesus of overcoming the chaos and transforming it into new creation fuelled the expectations of the early Christians for final (*eschaton*) revelation (*apocalypsis*) with the second coming of Jesus as the end of human history and of the world. Only gradually did they adjust to the tension between the finality of God's work involving the intrusion of the transhistorical *eschaton* and the time-laden human response still required in history. New creation is already and not yet. It does not exist in some state of suspended animation but its creative validity must be expressed in the confinement and vulnerability of cosmic time and human history. To invoke another powerful scriptural metaphor, the kingdom of God has come and is yet to come.

Cosmos and humanity, despite the ineradicable presence of kingdom and new creation, remain vulnerable to the return of desert and chaos. Such returns may now prove, in the logic of Calvary, fresh sources of Kingdom presence and re-creation The creative pattern of Calvary operates in the personal life and death of each human being. It has its analogies in the histories of human societies and cultures and even in the rhythms and perhaps destiny of the cosmos itself.

The development of life and its disintegration in death, characteristic of our planet, reveals the dynamism inherent in creation, the movement from chaos or formlessness to form and creation and back to formlessness again. That humans endure this themselves and compound or even cause it for other beings, human and non-human, constitutes the tragic element in human experience. Human ability and inclination to destroy on a vast scale, to the point of reducing the whole planet to chaos today, confirms humanity's fatal flaw and the earth's fatal vulnerability. The history of twentieth-century war, (cf. chapters 2 and 14 of this work) and the radical intensity of the programme to annihilate the Jews (ch. chapters 6 and 7), underline the contemporary human capacity for self-destruction and the destruction of others. On a local Irish level, as Part II and particularly chapters 10 and 11 indicate, human destructiveness finds its own Irish form. Yet the Christian resources for new creation, precisely in and through disintegration and destruction of personal life, freedom and even faith, as well as of Church, society and civilisation, continue to assert themselves. Various chapters examine this dialectic in terms of faith (chapter 3) and freedom (chapter 4), of peace and justice (chapter 5), of forgiveness (chapter 6) and wider sacramental energy (chapter 7). How fringe societies (chapter 2) and people (chapter 13) like the man from Nazareth, become resources for new creation is part of the justification for doing theology at the fringe.

Fringe Theology and the Centre God

Theology needs to look more closely at its precisely theological resource, the presence of the God of Genesis and Golgotha at the heart of human destruction and failure. In Israel's experience of failure and destruction, its major

6

resource and consolation was the fidelity of its God, Yahweh, his fidelity to his promises and to his people. Acknowledgment of this fidelity was frequently put to the test, both for the people as a whole, as the psalms testify, and for individuals such as Job. Divine fidelity and Israel's trust in it prevailed. *Emeth* (amen) proved the dominant characteristic of a faithful and patient God and it called for imitation, even emulation, from a sometimes impatient and unfaithful people.

The fidelity of God to his people despite their failure, his patience in face of their rejection, assumed the form of compassion or co-suffering. This co-suffering or suffering with emerged as a form of pro-suffering or suffering for, by anticipation in the suffering servant of Isaiah and by participation in the suffering Son, Jesus. Taking on the sins of humanity in Jesus, God takes on the sufferings of the world. He accepts, is inhabited by the sufferings of all the world's victims (cf. chapters 7 and 11). 'Come to me all you who labour and are burdened.' And he remains in reconciling solidarity with the victimisers of the world: 'Father forgive them.' Victims and victimisers, and so many people are both, human beings are never abandoned by God. Knocking at the heart of each, offering consolation, calling for repentance, is the God who has taken on the human condition in all its destructiveness.

The compassionate and co-suffering, forgiving and reconciling God is continually doing a new creative thing. His inexhaustible resources were most fully revealed on Calvary; that utter weakness and chaos were symbol and source of new power and new creation. The infinite power of God is revealed as his inexhaustible loving solidarity with human beings and his inexhaustible creativity transforming death into life and chaos into new creation. The pattern continues of human suffering and human destructiveness encountering the co-suffering inexhaustible and creative God in life and liturgy (chapter 8), in the chilling counter-sacrament of the Holocaust (chapter 7) and in the aspiration to and fragile experience of freedom (chapters 4 and 14).

The vocation of human beings is to imitate the faithful and creative God by allowing his presence and resources to transform them from within and to find expression in their personal and social lives. The 'instress', to adapt Hopkins's

7

terms, of the pressure and presence within creation and within human beings of this inexhaustible God is to shape their lives in 'inscape'. Social and cultural patterns are also called to manifest this 'grandeur of God', even as they continue in their ambiguity to manifest so much of human folly and evil.

Bekan, Babylon and Beyond

In the sheltered environment of the fringe Irish village of Bekan, County Mayo, where I grew up, faith in the creative, saving God was taken for granted. Our truly fringe existence left us without a policeman, a public-house or a Protestant within the confines of a large rural parish. So a crime-free, sober and Catholic life-style seemed inevitable and unassailable. Yet there was a growing desert, only gradually visible to youthful eyes, as so many contemporaries in those formative years in the 1930s and 1940s had to leave village, county and country in search of work, and some of those who stayed behind were condemned to be lonely spinsters and bachelors.

Revival of parish life had to wait for the 1960s and 1970s and then on a more prosperous but much less populous scale. For those who stayed, it came very late. For those who left for what must have seemed to timorous Bekan eyes a version of Babylon, new life and new creation became possible in Britain and the United States, even Africa and Asia. Despite our village voices, emigration and mission had given us universal horizons beyond Bekan or Babylon. Awareness of the harshness of life had made it possible to recognise features of Babylon operating in Bekan also.

A deeper sense of human dignity and of Christian mystery confirmed that the village on the periphery is as much the centre of the world as Babylon or Rome, London or Washington. Patrick Kavanagh was already proclaiming this in his poem 'Epic' among others:

> I have lived in important places, times
> When great events were decided, who owned
> That half a rood of rock, a no-man's land
> Surrounded by our pitchfork-armed claims.
> I heard the Duffys shouting 'Damn your soul'

8

And old McCabe stripped to the waist, seen
Step the plot defying blue cast-steel —
'Here is the march along these iron stones'
That was the year of the Munich bother. Which
Was more important? I inclined
To lose my faith in Ballyrush and Gortin
Till Homer's ghost came whispering to my mind
He said: I made the Iliad from such
A local row. Gods make their own importance.

In Christian terms, which Kavanagh shared so deeply, the divine importance of Nazareth and Calvary illuminates the significance of peripheral places like Bekan. The Eucharist celebration of the mysteries of Nazareth and Calvary in the villages of the world makes them centre and source for Christ's new creation, which will finally prevail but is often obscured by rural desert and urban slum, sacraments of chaos.

The Theological Pilgrimage

For many years I have been attempting to explore the relation between faith and ethics in principle and in various fields of human behaviour. This volume is intended to continue this work but for the most part implicitly. The deeper dialectic of Christian existence struggling between chaos and new creation has thrust itself forward and the more urgent and neglected relation between universal and local theology has begun to press its claims. Theology as autobiography moves inexorably on.

PART I

Confronting the Modern World

2.

Gospel and Culture

THERE is no need to emphasise the impossible range of this topic. The limited aspects discussed here were chosen partly from a concern at their neglect in certain theological discussions of Vatican II's great charter *Gaudium et Spes* and partly because of the particular European perspective which Europe's outermost western isle may offer. Ireland is European, much more now than in the nineteenth or early twentieth century, much less perhaps than in the seventh and eighth centuries. Yet the view from the fringe has its own advantages, and the fringe or periphery its own gospel and cultural prophets as we shall see.

With some sense of the geography of this essay one may turn to the history, which will dominate. Two rather general and introductory remarks about the historical setting are necessary although they will not be developed here. The approach of the year 2000, of the end of the second millennium of Christianity, will have much influence, both superficial and profound, on the shape of our thinking and analysis, religious and secular, over the next decade. Some of this influence will have a millenarian and apocalyptic quality. The end of the millennium is bound to have echoes of the end of a civilisation, of Christianity perhaps, even of humanity. Conveniently (if that is the *mot juste*) we have the very instruments to hand which could produce apocalypse now and we may well have, too, the situation and the leaders to decree it. The shadow of the bomb, of human annihilation by human or divine decree, will lie heavily on Gospel message and cultural activity in the years ahead, intensifying the darkness of the

13

inevitable millenarianisms. Such darkness and the fear it inspires will find fundamentalist interpreters, both religious and political, from both left and right. In the renewed battles of these fundamentalists, the divine gifts of Gospel and the human achievements of culture will be critically at risk. The *spes* (hope) of Vatican II will be more necessary than ever to the Church in the modern world. The *gaudium* (joy) is likely to be more muted.

In a quite different historical mood one might find curious connections between the relationships of Gospel and culture, of Church and society in the late fourth and late twentieth centuries. In the age of Ambrose and Theodosius the Church was completing its transition from the catacombs to the basilicas. Church and Gospel had invaded and overcome the political establishment; the cultural establishment would be conquered in turn. But such conquests are never one-sided. In so many ways Gospel message, praxis and structures were in turn invaded and shaped by the Roman and Greek civilisation they appeared to conquer. One consequence of this mutual reshaping of Gospel and culture was the development, however reluctant, of a Christian justification of war. Confronting and apparently conquering the world of its time, the Gospel found itself having to accommodate the military responsibility which Christians had so long, for the Gospel's sake, refused. It may have been an unavoidable accommodation for late fourth-century Christians but its consequences have been long and fateful.

The connections with the late twentieth-century challenge to Gospel and Church may be focused on the issues of peace and war; nuclear and total war involving the superpowers or limited regional wars involving local liberation or conquest, though these are often surrogate expressions of the struggles between the superpowers. In the European and North American contexts where the dangers of nuclear war predominate, peace movements, frequently invoking Gospel authority, have greatly influenced the Churches in a move almost the reverse of that of the fourth century. In their documents on peace and war and particularly nuclear war, the Church of England Working Party and the US Conference of Catholic Bishops have signalled their move away from their traditional blessing of their governments' policies on war and defence. In third world countries

14

the movement away from association with government policies is marked by increased Church commitment to justice and human rights. A new relationship of the Gospel-bearing Church to government, state and society is emerging, a relationship quite different from the model first established at the end of the fourth century. Such a change will provide a new context for Gospel and culture, for that continuance or completion of incarnation known as 'inculturation'. Such interaction of Gospel and culture can never be sheer deduction from the fact or doctrine of incarnation any more than it can be uncritical surrender to the predominant cultural patterns of the place and time. The independence of the Churches on such crucial issues as peace and justice in society encourages the hope that interaction of Gospel and culture will be both critical and creative.

This chapter is, however, more particularly concerned with late twentieth-century Europe and how the Gospel-culture relationship may be developing there. In making an assessment of that, we must look again at the transforming experiences which Europe has undergone in this century. Every level of people's living and dying in Europe has been deeply affected by the negative experiences of two great wars. One of the surprising features of Vatican II and particularly of its document on the Church and the World, almost entirely European/North American in tone and context, was its ignoring of the great wars and their influence.

Two moments only on the war-history of twentieth century Europe will be considered. In them is revealed the destruction of the claims of Europe, European Christianity and European culture to world leadership and centrality. These two movements are the Holocaust and the end of Empire. However the Holocaust is evaluated and responded to by Jews, religiously, morally and politically, it provides profound challenges for Christians, particularly European Christians. These challenges are considered more fully elsewhere. It is a matter for some rejoicing that Vatican II responded indirectly to those Christian challenges in its document on non-Christian religions, *Nostra Aetate*. It is a matter for considerable regret that the Holocaust had not a more direct and explicit influence on the Council Fathers and theologians, so many of whom had lived with it and through it. If it had, the tragic dimension

15

of human life, essential to genuine Christian hope, would be more readily discernible in the Council documents, particularly in the constitution on the Church in the Modern World. I return to this in a later chapter.

The tragedy of the European Jews is also a tragedy of European Christians. It undermines utterly the long-cherished European Christian claims to religious and moral leadership. The brokenness of European Christians and Christianity revealed by the horrors of the Holocaust has yet to be appreciated and appropriated. Until it is, the new religious and moral life, the conversion which is necessary and possible, will be impeded and impoverished. The brokenness, accepted as such, is part of the necessary dying to sin and so rising to new life, which is essential Christian renewal. For now we Europeans are at least confronted with the incredibility of our previous, frequently implicit but no less real and always arrogant, claims to show the world the moral and religious way forward. The European Catholic Church in particular may find hard the lesson of its mid twentieth-century European experience that it has more to learn from the peripheral and underdeveloped peoples of the world than it has to teach.

The recognition of this moral and religious humiliation should come easier to a Europe which has lost its political and economic domination with the loss of its former empires. London, Paris, Rome and the other great European capitals no longer control the world's political stage, or the money-markets. They are no longer the centre of administration or even attention for the A-peoples of the world, Americans (North and South), Africans, Asians and Australasians. Europe, at least Western Europe, has moved to the periphery of many people's consciousness and interest, people for whom Europe was so long central when they were peripheral. The end of empire, of actual dominance, does not always mean the end of imperialism, the mentality of dominance. Yet the summons to realism, to the truth, is also Europe's opportunity, in Gospel terms *kairos*. To shed the privileges and claims of Empire is also to shed its burdens and inhibitions. It includes the prospect of liberation, enabling imperial people to become people, to rejoin the human community as equals, as partners rather than masters. With the loss of Europe's empires Europeans are free to appreciate and be

16

enriched by the humanity, traditions and achievements of peoples regarded as outside the gates and often described as barbarians. A barbarian may, however, be better described as somebody unwilling or unable to recognise and appreciate the values of another people and another culture. Within that description there may have been more barbarians within than outside the gates. Imperial voices often concealed barbarian attitudes. The fate of peoples, traditions and land exposed to European expansionism in the past involved a great deal of barbaric exploitation which is only gradually being recognised. (The new imperial peoples, east and west of Europe, seem destined to repeat many of Europe's mistakes without necessarily emulating European achievements.)

This attention to Europe's failure and Europe's loss is not intended as some indulgence in masochism or as an encouragement of neurotic and paralysing guilt-feelings. Indeed by confronting the evil and the loss, by accepting its new and humbler position, Europe's peoples may hope to contribute to the humanising of the world in ways which power and inevitable accompanying arrogance previously precluded.

In all this, major Christian themes seem continually about to surface. Europe, with its remarkable religious and cultural heritage from a past age continues to enrich the world through its political, economic and technological achievements. That creativity has by no means come to an end. European creativity developed its own promethean tendencies and imperialist activities which finally came to grief in the twentieth century. The fall of empires and civilisations is also illuminated by the stories of Genesis. And the experience of war, loss of power and prestige, even exile from the centre to the fringes of the world, can provide the purification and redemption which lead to fresh life and creativity, new creation.

Theologians are sometimes loath to move from individual understanding of Christian redemption to a broader canvas, involving people, society, civilisation or the totality of human history. There are obvious dangers in applying the great Jewish and Christian symbols to the historical life of even an individual. Yet if they are to be confined to some spiritual and ahistorical realm, they become both irrelevant and empty of meaning while clearly betraying their foundation in the his-

17

torical figures of Israel, Jesus and his disciples. And it is not possible to be historical even about the individual without being social. The isolated individual with a personal, a social history of salvation is an abstraction owing more to modern individualism than to Hebrew or Christian tradition. Jesus' message, like Israel's, was historical and social, as well as eschatological and personal. The Kingdom which he preached, promised and manifested was a social reality with historical expression. From Augustine to Gutiérrez, Christian theologians have attempted to come to terms with this. Reflection on recent European history in the light of the grand themes of creation, fall and redemption has its dangers and limitations and no doubt mistakes, but it is not simply an aberration from the central theological tradition.

A critical aspect of the new Europe must be the development of genuine hope. The temptation to hopelessness or sense of absurdity which affected some major European thinkers in this century had a real basis in experience. Irishman Samuel Beckett reflects that experience in his own particular and progressive way, in his preoccupation with the isolation, impoverishment, decline, even dismemberment of the human being. Yet I believe that while he has not proved able to say 'yes' to humanity, he has not finally said 'no' and may by now be incapable of saying it. He remains a constant reminder of the Gethsemane and Calvary dimensions of human existence. The recent history of Europe has innumerable Gethsemane and Calvary experiences to record. It they are not only recorded but appropriated and lived through, they can transcend shallow optimism and generate genuine Christian hope. Europe is ready for and in need of that hope although for some of its people it may be already excluded by the tranquillisers and distractions of a consumerist civilisation.

As real hope in Christian perspective must endure the test of suffering, so true power is found at the fringe, among the powerless. Moved from the centre at least in certain respects, Europe may be able to recover such a sense of the power of the powerless, the centrality of these at the periphery or in more Christian terms the subversion of powers and principalities and centres.

The man from Nazareth came from the fringe. He associated mainly with the outsiders and the powerless. He fell victim to

18

the powerful, religious and political, at the centre in Jerusalem. His destruction outside the gates was parallel to the destruction of the Temple, the centre, all centres. 'Neither in this place nor in Jerusalem' but 'wherever two or three are gathered together in my name'... 'In the breaking of bread' the Emmaus disciple recognised him. The bread of life is the heart of the community, the heart of the world, the only centre which counts. *Ubi Eucharistia, ibi Ecclesia, ibi Christus, ibi Cosmos, ibi Deus.* Where the Eucharist is, there is the Church, the Christ, the Cosmos, God. In a wayside church, in a family home, at the bedside of the dying, in prison, at sea — this Eucharist, the centre, can happen anywhere and does.

The recent experience of Europe has been a decentring experience. Such experience can be revealing of the true significance of Jesus' transformation of human relations and power structures. The movable centre of Jesus himself and his footwashing exercise of power allow us Europeans to move more easily and freely in a world in which the weight of armour and other aspects of the 'white man's burden' restricted us for so long.

Of course I write as a fringe European although, if there are no centres there are, properly speaking, no fringes. Earlier I referred to fellow-Irishman Samuel Beckett who has worked at the margins of human existence in his novels and plays. His tramps and isolates still speak of life, if increasingly of very minimal life for these marginal individuals. They do not, as I said, finally say no.

His friend and compatriot, James Joyce, who had a more revolutionary impact on European literature and culture, operated in a very different idiom. His 'hero' was a city, a fringe city, Dublin. Central to his great novel of that city, *Ulysses*, was the fringe character of Leopold Bloom, lonely Jew in a teeming Catholic city. The fringe element might be explored more fully but the impact of the novel in its loud, exhilarating response to life is expressed in the final words, 'Yes, I will, yes.'

The not quite 'No' of Beckett and the exultant 'Yes' of Joyce encompass the darkness and light, the death and new life of twentieth-century Europe. Despite their own distance from the Gospel, their contribution to European culture

19

reveals much of the creativity and creation, promethean pride and fall, redemption and resurrection which in Christian symbols continue to express the deeper life of humanity and its cultures.

3.

The Grace of Unbelief

KARL RAHNER's 'anonymous Christian' is widely interpreted to mean that everyone is a crypto-believer, indeed a crypto-Christian believer. There is something to be said for reversing the thesis and saying every Christian believer is a crypto-unbeliever. More precisely one might argue that each Christian believer carries within, an unbelieving *alter ego*. This shadow side of faith may seem too threatening if acknowledged explicitly, even to oneself. Yet properly addressed it can provide a fruitful tension within the believer and the believing community. So far from undermining faith, the thrust to unbelief may help faith grow. One may fairly speak, in those circumstances, of fruitful tension and growth, of the 'grace of unbelief'.

Keeping Faith Honest

An unbelieving friend occasionally remarks *a propos* our religious positions: 'We need each other to stay honest' (he in his unbelief, I in my belief). But one's own unbelieving tendencies can and frequently do summon one's faith to account. This may be particularly true of theologians. Thomas Mann's remark that writers are people who find it very difficult to write might well be adapted to describe theologians as people who find it very difficult to believe. Their vocation demands that they take the objections to Christian belief seriously. Their responsibility is not just to their own faith but to the faith of the Church. Part of that responsibility is to keep the Church's faith honest. The troubles theologians encounter are sometimes related to their poor or powerful efforts to discharge that part of their responsibility, keeping the Church's faith honest. A recent, and by now perhaps uncontroversial, example was the ban imposed on the American Jesuit theologian, John Courtney Murray, for his writings on religious liberty in the 1950s. He survived to become the chief architect of the Church's own position with Vatican II's *Declaration on Religious Liberty* in the early 1960s. Not all theological attempts to keep the faith honest, truthful to the teaching of the gospel, the tradition of the Church and the needs of the time, have been as meritorious or as successful. And of course keeping faith honest is not a task confined to theologians.

Each believer faces temptations, often subtle or disguised, to accommodate his faith and his God to some need or convenience in ways ultimately unfaithful. Temptations to intellectual dishonesty haunt more than theologians in pursuit of a career in Church or university, captive to a particular constituency in society or just concerned for a comfortable life. The Church at large has suffered from the corruption of intellectual dishonesty at times, as various leaders and teachers placed lower-level concerns of, say, 'not disturbing the faithful' and so creating difficulties for the clergy, before openness to the truth. It may take a coalition between the unbelieving criticism of outsiders and the sceptical fidelity of insiders before the community reaches a richer and purer faith, as it did for example in regard to the relation between the Genesis account of creation and the theory of evolution or the kerygmatic character of the gospels and the contemporary understanding of history. Of course the process of interaction was two-way in relating Genesis and evolution, gospels and history. Crude positions on both sides were modified and refined. The 'believer' in evolution or in contemporary historical method needed to have his own lurking unbelief stimulated. Religious believers are not the only believers tempted to suppress the nagging doubt. As my atheist friend maintains, to stay honest he needs theists as friends, including the theist in his own closet.

It would be mistaken to think of faith's temptations to dishonesty in exclusively intellectual terms. Faith as a way of life proves so demanding that most of us fail much of the time in varying degrees. There is no escaping a certain objective dishonesty in the gap between what we believe and preach and what we do. The danger is that subjectively we will seek to ignore it. The Pharisee who went up to the temple to pray is no stranger in Christian circles, particularly when we are rejoicing that we are not like him. The comfortable assumption of virtue by so many comfortable Christians indicates some serious failure in measuring the following of Jesus Christ against the standards of his call, some dishonesty in faith as way of life.

The extent of that failure is becoming increasingly evident in the acceptance, at least passive, by privileged Christians of the inhuman conditions of the deprived. Faith as the following of Jesus Christ demands sharing in his mission to the excluded and deprived. Where it has not been shamefully hijacked to protect privilege by spiritualising privation with deferment of fulfilment to the next world, faith has yet to meet fully the challenge to honesty which the historical and social expression of salvation and liberation, of the coming of the kingdom and love of neighbour, poses. The present structure of society, national and international, with its divisions and exploitations, constitutes a clear countersign to Jesus and his mission. Acceptance of that society by people who also proclaim their acceptance of Jesus involves contradiction and dishonesty. The unbeliever Marx and his many unbelieving followers have helped to formulate that challenge for Christians. The unbeliever in the Christian is also sceptical of the formulations and the practice of faith in such a divided and destructive world. He asks: who benefits and who loses from such a formulation on, say, peace or justice? Whose interests are being served by involvement in, or rejection of, a particular practice? How far are salvation and liberation and the other great Christian symbols and doctrines being manipulated in favour of power or wealth or pleasure or any of the other false gods of these and other times? His sceptical, unbelieving self keeps him alert to the deeper idolatries which can infiltrate and disfigure true faith. It is only by listening to and attempting to respond to this unbelieving self that the continuing temptation to worship false gods which affects Christians, as it did Israel, may be overcome and true faith survive.

The unbelieving *alter ego* is one who keeps asking the awkward questions. Bernard Lonergan sees in the human capacity and need to question, a radical openness that can never be completed or closed in history by historical answers. In this as in much else he comes close to his Jesuit *confrère*, Karl Rahner, for whom the openness of the human being to the transcendent mystery is given its correct historical and specific form through faith in the God of Jesus Christ. Questioning is the way to faith. At least the capacity and drive to go on questioning excludes captivity to the godlings of history. The ultimate, ungraspable mystery is always summoning and, in Jewish and Christian tradition, empowering us to follow Abraham, our father in faith, and move on. A living faith means living with questions. The sceptical disturber of the faith, who surfaces from time to time even in the secure believer, is part of the summons and the grace to leave the security of complete answers and of a reduced God. Faith, despite the echo of cliché, is a journey, a pilgrimage, a moving on. The God to whom we respond is ahead of us, towards whom we move. To keep on the move we need the stimulus of questions and of quest. The movement of faith is a search for the God who calls us. Faith as search means living with questions, not suppressing them. Living with questions means recognising the quizzical, sceptical, unbelieving self who is to be cherished as our constant companion in the search for God. Without that sceptical companion we may easily settle for a God fashioned more and more in our own image. The real difficulty with the fundamentalist, in scripture, in doctrine, in authority, is not simply that he disallows certain questions and suppresses the sceptical self; but in doing so he prevents the fuller emergence of God. He refuses the risks of God's own summons. He refuses and distorts God. Fundamentalism, for all its self-righteous claims to faithfulness and orthodoxy, is fundamentally unfaithful and can only issue in unorthodoxy, incorrect understanding of the God who called Abraham and Moses and Jesus Christ.

The fundamentalist who refuses to live with questions has his counterpart in the total sceptic or agnostic who refuses to live with any answers. Both, however personally sincere, are refusing the human call to and capacity for truth. The sceptic refuses to accept the truth available with all its limitations and its demands to be corrected and transcended. He does not listen, at least in religious matters, to the believer in himself. Of course he could not conduct his life in general if the believer in himself, who accepts various truths and trusts an indefinite number of people, did not in practice prevail in most of his life. His 'principled' stand on religious doubt fits uneasily into his ready acceptance of so much else. Without attempting to explore the psychological and social background to the scepticism of any, it is important to see its oddity in the context of the trust, even credulousness, so many religious sceptics display in other areas. More deeply, such scepticism can, objectively, without attributing blame, reveal a refusal of responsibility. In our twilit world we have the responsibility to accept and live by the truth available and not seek to evade that in the name of intellectual purity. Living with the limited answers available, while conscious of their limitations, is as much an obligation as living with the questions which underline the limitations.

The recent emphasis on praxis and orthopraxis in understanding and evaluating faith could help to overcome a certain self-indulgent preoccupation with how far one believes and in which doctrine. The divine call to faith expressed in Jesus Christ is a call to follow, to a life of discipleship, to doing the truth in love and service of the neighbour. Delicate debate about the meaning of the virgin birth or theological pluralism can seem very precious and irrelevant to people faced with the personal and social challenges of the Calcutta of Mother Teresa or the Recife of Bishop Helder Camara. Living and doing Christianity, in response to life and death needs, becomes a more searching and valid test of faith than any critical intellectual activity. The witness of love even unto death is the proper expression of faith and the most effective answer to sceptics.

Yet such witness in life and death is witness to truth, a doing of truth. Orthopraxis may not be separated from orthodoxy. Intellectual analysis and debate must accompany loving service, if that service is to be really truthful and so properly loving. Too many people have died for too many bizarre and destructive causes to justify any split between love

25

and truth. The joy of genuine martyrs must not be obscured by the hysteria of Jonestown. For that patient intellectual analysis and the presentation of truth by which Christians live and die are essential. Orthopraxis and orthodoxy enjoy equiprimacy. Unquestioned and unquestioning activity is no more effective guide to the God ahead than unquestioned and unquestioning assertion. The sceptical self has to raise awkward questions about the actions of faith just as much as about its beliefs. The answers of Christian praxis have to live with the challenge of these sceptical questions.

Growth in Faith

Faith on the move does not experience straightforward progress. While faith changes in the course of life, that change, for person or community, is not simple development or decline. Charting the course of changing faith for Church or believer is a complex and subtle task. Of interest here is the role of the sceptical, unbelieving self in that change where it issues in growth.

The Christian believer and community see faith as response to the God who addresses them, who communicates the divine self to them, who is present to them and in them. It is the presence which calls forth and enables the faith response. Presence and response are finally divine gift. This understanding of faith and presence relates contemporary experience to the experiences of Israel and of Jesus. Their experiences form the standard of interpretation within the living tradition in which Christian believers are introduced to the presence of God and the response of faith.

The breakthrough to humankind by God in Israel and Jesus reaches successive generations in the community of word and sacrament. The breakthrough is partial, fitful, ambiguous in its reception by individuals and communities. The divine presence in history is undeniable but the limitations of history render it obscure, reduce its impact and frequently distort it. Human beings, their languages and relationships, their structures and activities, can bear little enough of the divine reality. Only through these languages and relationships, structures and activities can the divine presence reach us, can we respond to it. At our most receptive, when we are most fully open to the Spirit of God, these human forms will soar to unparalleled heights of expression in truth and love. In the poetry of Isaiah in the theology of Aquinas and in the joyous poverty of Francis may be found some more adequate traces of the breakthrough which reached its historical completion in Jesus Christ.

Breakdown or Breakthrough?

The questioning, sceptical self may well provide a crisis of faith. This can be frightening for the individual concerned and even more so for people who accept some responsibility for the faith of others, bishops, priests, teachers, parents. It may prove cold consolation in a particular case to suggest that loss of faith in general may be due to too little rather than too much questioning, to the movement, under fashionable pressure, from uncritical acceptance to uncritical abandonment. Unless questioning is not only tolerated but encouraged and even structured into education in the faith, growth and maturity of a critical faith are impossible and the capacity to resist the superficial attractions of modish unbelief remains undeveloped.

Structural questioning, for all its value, cannot anticipate the impact of certain harsh realities. The premature death of a parent or a spouse or a child cannot be prepared for in textbook fashion. The scandals of world poverty or of totalitarianism of left and right, of racism in South Africa or of injustice and violence in Ireland may suddenly penetrate even sophisticated defences. What kind of God presides over this kind of world? What kind of faith allows so many believers to tolerate or even benefit from this kind of evil? The God and the faith of an earlier, innocent age are confronted by the believer's own loss of innocence. Destruction and hatred abound. They seem to be as characteristic of religious believers, Christian and other, as of unbelievers. Is God still credible and faith still possible? The impact of these and other experiences can result in a breakdown in faith. The believer is no longer able to accept the God of previous experience and education. The choice lies between crucial development and abandonment, between continuing breakdown and breakthrough. Despite its personal particularity for the individual

27

and the occasion, the phenomenon of breakdown and of the stark choices it presents has a long history in Israel and Church. The founding fathers and documents of Jewish faith faced such choices as, for example, Abraham and the sacrifice of Isaac, Moses and his burden of leading his people out of Egypt, Job with the tormentors, a whole people in exile. The temptations which Jesus faced in the desert, more subtly in his ministry and crucially in the garden and on the cross, reveal the depth of the challenge to faith as response to the *real* God. The breakdown of Jesus abandoned unto death proved the necessary gateway to the breakthrough of resurrection. Jesus' death and resurrection provide the true way into understanding the meaning and the risk of growth in faith through breakdown and breakthrough.

The breakdown which faith may face could be too readily interpreted in intellectual terms. The difficulties of Abraham and Moses and Jesus did not take that narrowly intellectual form. The waves of doubt which wash over most of us from time to time come from much less articulate sources than the philosophy debates at school. And they are not always related to a particular crisis. Carrying the flotsam and jetsam of a life lived on the near side of chaos, the waves, which threaten to submerge us, may be waves of meaninglessness or hopelessness or apathy. A distaste for Church or faith or God, sudden or cumulative, may lack any precise cause but lead us to seek release from the burdens of belief. Unbelief as liberation is a tempting prospect for the conscientious and harassed as well as for the self-indulgent.

A certain kind of self-indulgence attempts to replace our tenuous and partial understanding and acceptance of God with a certitude and completeness that ultimately reduce God. All believers are open to the temptation to domesticate God. So our partial understanding turned total, requires to be shaken if it is to be faithful to the real God. It is this God who is faithful to us who provides the shaking as he provides the faith. The unbelief which shatters our easy grip on a reduced God is the beginning of growth.

The presence of God is the final guarantee against the reduction of God and of faith. That presence may erupt in question and doubt against the cosiness and comfort of a God possessed. At their best our lives, relationships and

28

structures, which enter into the reality of our faith, are unable
to cope with the God they would express. God's attempts at
self-expression in human history have in Jewish and Christian
understanding encountered continuous breakdown. But the
breakdowns have also been breakthroughs, definitively in
Jesus' death and resurrection. In our personal and social
histories the breakdowns continue. God cannot find adequate
expression. Our faith as recognition and response remains
partial and distorted. The disruptive presence of God calls us
beyond the current limits. Breakdown will occur. But breakthrough is on offer. The shadow of the cross can yield to the
light of resurrection.

Interdependence

We become and develop as believers in community, in dependence on one another. We share faith and unfaith. Difficulties,
doubts and disbelief are no more individual than faith is. The
believing community is always in various ways an unbelieving
community. The criticism of Israel made by the prophets as
well as by Jesus, exposes the unbelieving side of God's first
people. Yet the community of believers, for all its ambiguity,
is a source of support and growth for us in our unbelieving
phases. At times a particular belief may seem particularly
repellent — say, hell; or particularly irrelevant — say, the
sacrament of Confirmation; or particularly meaningless —
say, indulgences. We cannot take on an investigation of the
whole of received doctrine at any one time. Even if we could
and did, the results (of a lifetime's work?) would not necessarily be conclusive. Yet we may not feel we can simply hand
the whole question of doctrines over to the hierarchy or the
theologians. One of the difficult doctrines may be precisely
the role of hierarchy or theologians. Hierarchy and theologians
may have their own difficulties. Acceptance of the community
and by the community are critical here. People who recognise
the particular community as a community of faith, as their
community of faith, commit themselves to discovering and
developing the fuller content of that faith in community.
That commitment may well coexist with difficulties about
particular doctrines without thereby excluding people from
the community. The assent to the presence of God in saving

truth in that community and so to taking its doctrines seriously as expressions of that truth, together with the commitment to the search for fuller understanding and acceptance of that truth, provide the basis for dynamic membership. The community and its leaders must recognise the basic faith commitment of such a believer and seek to provide the support, care and challenge required. Orthodoxy interacts with orthopraxis, the commitment to search for and live the fuller truths of faith, to provide a more comprehensive test of authentic membership.

The more pervasive doubts and difficulties may have little to do with doctrinal detail. God, Jesus and the Church provide, in that order, not just a hierarchy of truth but a hierarchy of doubt. It is within the believing and doubting community that we may hope to dissolve the doubt in a larger faith, to turn breakdown into breakthrough. The patience and sensitivity of this current community are essential for this. The community's acceptance of the doubting members as authentic seekers only makes sense in those members' acceptance of the authentic faith of the community as a whole. On that faith the doubters may rest from the struggle, find support and guidance.

The current community is not the fullness of the believing community. The faith and doubt of those who have gone before can provide the inspiration and model for contemporary struggles. The biblical and later Christian heroes, the saints, remain sources of understanding and comfort as long as their stories are not distorted by a false sense of reverence. In his recent book, *The Courage to Doubt*, Robert Davidson explores critical people and events of the Old Testament as they reveal the struggle between faith and doubt. A similarly realistic study of other figures and epochs would relieve many people from the guilt of doubt and so enable them to grow into fuller faith.

The past and present believing community has an openness to and responsibility to the future. Their God is a God of the future. Their faith is a faith for the future. Care for future generations demands a living faith now. A faith scrupulous about forms but lacking life will not help our children's children. The questions which life poses to faith have to be faced for the sake of future believers. Contem-

30

porary doubts and unbelief may not be avoided or deferred without a break in our fidelity to the future on the grounds that certain answers will last our time. The judgments we are tempted to make about Church failures in the sixteenth and nineteenth centuries should remind us of our perilous situation in the present. The dependence of future generations on the authenticity and largeness of our faith will make them critical judges of their inheritance.

Service, Praise and Patience

The journey of faith with its wrong turnings, retracings, blind alleys and uncertain progress could become self-destructive and self-absorbing. There are so many to attend to on the way that Jesus equiparated attention to others with recognition of himself, with faith (Mt. 25). Faith is a service of God and neighbour, of God in neighbour, a service of love. The living faith of love of neighbour is expressed in care and attention above all to 'the least ones' (Mt. 25). The business of serving, of doing the truth to those in need, is a necessary protection against self-indulgent agonising over particular intellectual forms of truth. Indeed the doing is not just the application of truth; it enters into the discovery of truth. In the faith of disciples of Jesus above all, recognition of truth is inextricably bound up with doing it. Activist, mindless doing is, of course, one escape route: inactive intellectual agonising is another. Theory and praxis, as the current jargon puts it, belong together in the thoughtful serving which Christians call faith.

Too busy to be, to be oneself, to sit still and be, to stop and savour being, to give thanks for it, to praise the author of our being and living and serving: that is not the Christian way of faith. The thanking, praising, worshipping character of Jewish and Christian traditions calls us to task from the struggles of believing and the frustrations of serving. To give thanks for where we are, for where we have come from and for where we are going, does not ignore the hurts of the past or fears of the future. It does not automatically expel doubt. It does meet our need to recognise gift and cry out thanks lest we be put to shame by the very stones. Celebration and praise take us beyond ourselves. When authentic they form a

31

breakthrough. When we feel more like breakdown, the community capacity for joy and wonder may still reach us and be all the more compelling and expanding for the reluctant, disbelieving mood in which they find us.

Service and praise will shorten the journey. They cannot of themselves hasten the arrival of the final destiny. God's coming in glory for all of us or for any one of us. So to be faithful is to be patient, to wait upon the Lord who comes when He will. Trying to anticipate, to force upon history, personal or social, the eschaton, the final culmination, is attempting to do violence to God. This is not a listless waiting. It must always be alert and attentive. Sometimes indeed it is busy in serving and noisy in song. But always it is waiting, trusting, accepting. The final temptation to unbelief, ambiguously conveyed by Beckett's tramps, Didi and Gogo, is to abandon all hope of his coming. Final and yet ambiguous because there is still the disbelief which may lead one beyond the captive God of one's need to the real God of Calvary and resurrection. The grace of doubt and unbelief makes room for that divine disruption whereby history becomes saving history.

4.

Set Free for Freedom
— Paul's Letter to the Galatians

IT IS NOT that the devil has the best lines but that the best words undergo the worst corruptions. *Corruptio optimi* ... The case-history of 'love' is notorious. It could happen to any rich and serious word. It has happened endlessly to 'freedom'. The current possibility of the 'freedom-loving' nations of the West and 'peace-loving' nations of the East totally destroying one another and the world, reveals the extensive corruption of two great words. Crimes committed in the name of freedom from Ballykelly to Beirut, Kabul and San Salvador make it increasingly difficult to engage in discussion of freedom or liberation or emancipation without provoking cynicism or apathy. Theologians and the Churches may not readily adopt a holier than this world attitude to the discussion. The fact that freedom is a great Christian and theological as well as human and worldly word cannot obscure the Church's own failures to protect and promote freedom in the course of its history. The Inquisition may be untypical and often unfairly presented. There is a history of 'fear of freedom' as a dominant Church attitude which still recurs today. This is where Paul and the Galatians provide a continuing judgment on and stimulus to our understanding and practice of Christian freedom.

Paul 'riles easy'. A few sentences into his letter to the Galatians (Celtic in origin) he is hurling anathemas. Ironically his anathema for 'those who would preach another Gospel', frequently invoked by later 'conservatives', is directed against the conservative 'Judaisers' who wish to impose the demands of Jewish law on Gentile Christians. This is the *casus belli* of the letter. Paul had checked this out at Jerusalem. Later he had to confront Peter about it at Antioch. The law does not apply to the Gentiles. Justification, salvation, liberation is not by law but by faith. It is therefore not a human but a divine achievement by God in Jesus Christ. Set free by Jesus, sharing in the promise of freedom to Abraham and his seed, shall the Galatians now exchange new freedom for old slavery? The reproofs and the arguments, the appeals to scripture and experience, the vision opened up of human freedom and unity, all this comes tumbling from Paul's passionate pen. He had come a sick man to the Galatians with this message of faith and freedom and had been enthusiastically received by then. Now in undoubtedly better health, indeed fighting fit, he must recall them to that original faith and freedom.

Beyond the Law and the Laws

The passion of Paul's rejection of the law and his defence of freedom for the Christian might appear naïve to the word-weary, even freedom-weary Christians of today. The sophistication of his theological argument and the realism of his vision of the world ought to dispel the suspicion of *naïveté.* Yet the burden of history, of Church law and practice, make us hesitant to share his enthusiasms. Were legal requirements of Judaism that much more extensive and inhibiting than subsequent Church laws? And where have the liberated Christians been all these centuries? Devices of rhetoric perhaps, but useful reminders of how much we need to recover the Pauline vision of Christians as a people set free and the Pauline passion in upholding that vision.

A people set free from the law certainly, from the trivial requirements of a fussy bureaucracy which never quite disappears. The days when a hatless priest in Galway was taken to be a Tuam priest have gone. Clerical presence in the wings at the Abbey seems scarcely credible today. These were the *trivia*. No doubt others persist and new ones emerge. Paul's critical view of his apostolic colleagues in surrendering to Jewish legalism provides a permanent basis for scrutinising Church laws and regulations, their number and detail.

Multiplicity and triviality of law, for all their erosion of Christian freedom, were not Paul's prime target. That was the status of law as way of achieving salvation. By observance of law, people aspired to justify themselves in the sight of God, to save themselves. (Echoes here of the Pharisee and the Publican.) This of course is 'another Gospel' (1:7). Faith not law is the way of justification (2:16, *passim*). The achievement is divine not human. In Jesus Christ, the promise made to Abraham and his seed is fulfilled (3:6 ff.) The faith of Abraham anticipated Christian faith in accepting God's initiative and achievement. The complex arguments about Abraham's seed as singular (Jesus Christ) and his true posterity (the Christians) as children of the free woman, Sarah (3:16 f.; 4:21-31) reinforce (and obscure) basic Pauline themes, developed more fully, for example, in his letter to the Romans. Justification, salvation is the free gift of God. Faith is the human way of acceptance. By that acceptance Christians are set free from the law and the other traditional slaveries of sin and of death (Romans).

The evangelical questions remain strange to Catholic ears: Are you saved? Have you been born again? Have you received the Spirit? Yet they reflect something of the thrust of Paul's concerns with the primacy and totality of the divine achievement in addressing the Galatians. The terminology of freedom, more akin to Paul's usage and thought here, tends to be used in more secular contexts such as the struggle for liberation, the emancipated or liberated woman, the free spirit, the independent mind. For Paul the divine achievement of human liberation is not confined to religious issues or some condition beyond history and out of this world, as will presently appear. The 'liberationists' and 'independents' capture an essential aspect of his message. The temptation to self-justification by observance of the law continues to trouble Christians and may assume strongly religious trappings. In its extreme forms it may paralyse the scrupulous. In a particularly unattractive form it issues in the self-righteousness of the respectable. In middle-class and clerical life this is our greatest temptation. The self-righteousness may easily slide into power-consciousness, not least because power is usually given to the respectable and so acceptable. However the power transfer occurs, the desire to rule, to regulate, to legislate has affected Christian leaders in ways similar to secular leaders. Despite Jesus' warning not to behave as secular rulers the temptation has frequently proved too much.

In the spate of regulations and efficiency of administration the freedom of the Christian finds little room for expression and development. There are many Church leaders who see themselves as promoters and protectors of authentic Christian freedom. Authentic, as so often, is the catch. Without people and structures to test the authenticity leaders can easily deceive themselves about their commitment to freedom. Paul confronting Peter at Antioch in the name of freedom (2:11) still constitutes an unusual Church event. The promise of collegiality and co-responsibility throughout the Church, which emerged after Vatican II, still provides hope of a leadership and collaboration dedicated to the development of a freed and free people, the people of God. The Synod of Bishops, the Pastoral Council of England and Wales, the open collegial style of many bishops' conferences — for example, South African, the development of lay commissioners, the diocesan assemblies of clergy, are all indications, however limited, that the free collaboration of a free people can give effective voice to Paul's message of Christian freedom.

The close link between freedom and community in Paul's vision reaches its climax in his famous reversal of the contemporary Jewish prayer in which the male Jew gave thanks that he was born neither Gentile nor slave nor female. For Paul 'there is neither Jew nor Greek, there is neither slave nor free, there is neither male nor female. For you are all one in Christ Jesus' (3:38). Traditional divisions based on race or religion, class or sex are undermined by God's action in Jesus Christ. The barriers must come down. A new kind of community is born. There is a new Israel, even a new Creation. Exodus and Genesis are superseded in the Kingdom inaugurated by Jesus and proclaimed by Paul.

The liberation for all captives, which Isaiah promised and Jesus announced (Is. 58:6; 61:1, 2; Lk. 4:16-21), applies to the Galatian Christians of about 50 AD. Attempts to restrict this by the Judaisers move Paul to his denunciation of privileges and barriers and his declaration of 'liberty, equality and fraternity' as characteristic of the new Israel, the new people of God.

The truly radical reform of human relationships accom-

36

plished in Jesus has always proved too much for human institutions. Paul was already struggling with this difficulty and sought to clarify it at least for the Galatians. Vatican II in various ways attempted to renew this Pauline vision. In the Constitution on the Church it moved from the Church as mystery of God's presence in the world (a divine not a human achievement) to the Church as people, sharing the radical equality of daughters and sons of the Father and so in chapter three to the service structures. As the secular philosophers and their political disciples discovered much later, liberty, including Christian liberty, emerges and develops in community (fraternity) and involves the mutual respect and acceptance of basic equality.

As the historical sign, embodiment and promoter of God's presence and saving power, of his Kingdom, the Church must realise and give witness to the freedom, equality and unity of human beings in Christ. In the recovered image of Vatican II, repeatedly invoked by Pope John Paul II, the Church is to be the sacrament, the sign and the realisation of the community of humankind with its essential accompaniments of freedom and equality. The work of salvation as work of liberation calls the Church to manifest in itself and promote in the world liberty, unity and equality.

Overcoming the divisions and enjoying the freedom were not to be recognised in principle and ignored in practice. And they were not to be relegated to the next world. They had to be fought for in this world in Galatia in 50 AD, in Ireland and a thousand other places in 1986 AD. There was a concrete content affecting the relations between Jew and Gentile, slave and free, man and woman.

The current vocabulary of political struggle speaks of 'liberated zones'. In the associated propaganda war one man's liberated zone is often another's occupied territory. In Paul's world of sin and slavery and law the Christian community was the liberated zone. The unfree world is still with us. The witness and reality of the liberated zone of the Church is as necessary as ever. How real is it? How evident is it?

The Church has a thousand angles. It offers a thousand perspectives. Recognising it as a 'liberated zone', community of the freed, involves angles and perspectives which differ for insider and outsider, associate and committed, cleric and

37

lay, bishop and priest. For quite other but powerful reasons, angle and perspective differ for rich and poor, for first, second and third worlds, for male and female. No one of these perspectives offers simple and complete truth. Yet one would hope — we are, as Paul might say, liberated in hope — that all angles and perspectives provide some evidence and experience of freedom. Do they?

The Experience of Freedom

Feeling free may not be the ultimate test of liberated Christians. In the historical community of the Church, laity ought normally and dominantly to feel free in relation to their priests, priests in relation to their bishops, theologians in regard to their clerical and episcopal Christian colleagues, women in regard to men. The 'feeling free' involves mutual respect, acceptance, trust. It involves a mutuality and equality which is not always evident, encouraged or even recognised. To recognise and encourage such mutual acceptance and trust it is necessary to provide the context, the continuous and frequently small-scale contact and community in which people can discover, express and develop their freedom. Paul's churches in Galatia and elsewhere provided this kind of context. Religious communities have institutionalised it, not always successfully. A rediscovery of it is recurring throughout the universal Church today in basic communities, particularly in the Third World and in a rich profusion of groups dedicated to prayer, peace and renewal. We need community support and structures to be free. That freedom involves participation in the work and decision-making of the community. Christian freedom as divine gift is mediated and expressed through Christian community. As mediated, freedom is caught, felt, assimilated in a community that knows itself to be free. As expressed, freedom develops the person and enriches the community. The creative works of Christian freedom renew the treasures of Christian community for new generations. In their liberated lives in the liberated zone of the Church, Christian laity and clergy offer to their contemporaries and successors the Spirit of freedom, whereby they were set free.

Personal Liberation

For Christian freedom and its witness communal structures like laws and institutions are important and necessary, but not, as the scientists say, sufficient. Paul was well aware of this. Personal conversion is as necessary as structural conversion. In the actual case of the Galatians the two were inextricably connected. To pretend to faith in Jesus while insisting on the old structures of the law for Gentiles involved self-contradiction. Paul was no less critical of personal self-indulgence on the pretext of freedom. The desires and works of 'the flesh' (unliberated man) are to be rejected and they exclude from the Kingdom of God. These include 'idolatry and sorcery', 'fornication and impurity', 'enmity, strife, jealousy and anger', 'drunkenness [and] carousing', and all forms of 'selfishness' (5:16-21). By contrast 'the fruit of the Spirit [of freedom] is love, joy, peace, patience, kindness, goodness, faithfulness, gentleness, self-control'.

These contrasting pictures of the licentious and liberated person draw attention to the personal structures of freedom and the personal conversion it involves. In another idiom the liberated person is the integrated person. Possibly diverging desires and powers come together in creative freedom. The licentious person remains unintegrated, with desires and powers fragmenting and conflicting. In the integrated but developing and dynamic, not static, person, the powers of creation fragmented by sin recover their direction and effectiveness. They become the powers of new creation. The liberated, free person acts out of these dynamic creative capacities, which have been traditionally called virtues.

Setting One Another Free

Paul's insight into the liberated Christian as integrated and virtuous does not imply some kind of self-contained, isolated, self-sufficient being. The freedom and independence of the Christian is not the autonomy of isolation but the freedom of gift and of interdependence. The gift from God and dependence on him is crucial to Paul. No less essential is the relationship with neighbour. Here (Gal. 5.14) as in the letter to the Romans (13:9) Paul summarises the whole Christian life as love of neighbour, taking the summary a stage beyond even Jesus. In loving the neighbour, service to the point of bearing his burdens becomes the test of fulfilling the new 'law of Christ' (6:2). Here Paul is returning to the recognition, acceptance and mutuality implicit in his understanding of the Christian community and its freedom from divisions.

The freedom for community and person is now more intimately and explicitly connected with love and service of the neighbour. It is through that love and service that Christians express and receive their freedom. We are set free for and by one another.

The mystery of incarnation will always challenge us. That God was in Jesus reconciling and liberating the world and humankind will always remain, for those who take it seriously, barely credible and almost totally incomprehensible. We need signs and wonders nearer home. Neighbours provide these. Neighbours are these. They too may call God, Abba, Father by the gift of the Spirit. They also constitute the liberating presence of God to us. In love and service of neighbours we are summoned out of ourselves. By mediating the presence of God to us they enable us to go out of ourselves. Set free for them we become our true selves. The mystery of incarnation is focused in the mystery of neighbour. The mystery of Christian liberation takes flesh in our love for one another. Our highest dignity and deepest challenge as Christians is to set one another free by this power of God manifested and realised in Jesus the Christ.

Paul's charter of freedom embraces our whole selves and our whole world. It is personal, political and cosmic. It is liberation in hope and liberation in history. The kingdom of the free is among us and still to come. In the community of the Church we dare to say: Our Father, who art among us, you have come to set us free. Our freedom, our commitment to the liberation of one another and of humankind is at once gift and call for us as it was for the Galatians. 'For freedom Christ has set us free; stand fast therefore and do not submit again to the yoke of slavery' (5:1).

5.

Peace-Makers
or Justice Seekers?

Disciples' Dilemma

In many contemporary situations people appear to be faced
with the choice of either seeking justice or making and maintaining peace. Where human rights have become the major
symbol of political justice, their promotion may be possible
only through armed revolution or at the very least by putting
the current social order at risk. South Africa provides a
notable example of this cruel dilemma which is experienced
all the more acutely by Christian disciples, called as they are
to be both justice-seekers and peace-makers (Mt. 5:6,9).
Various statements by South African church leaders and the
very considered and considerable *Kairos* document by South
African theologians give painful witness to this dilemma.

It operates elsewhere in varying forms. Indeed in the
world as a whole, a whole Church, which the Christian Church
is called to be, faces a world dilemma. In the affluent, dominant or first world of the West and North, where civil and
political rights are generally respected, the dominant threat
to humanity seems to be the threat of war, particularly
nuclear and total war, the war of annihilation. In the poor,
deprived third world, the more immediate threat seems to be
poverty and political oppression, the denial of economic,
social, political and civil rights. In the second world, mainly
Eastern Europe and communist countries, basic economic
and social needs are provided for, but political and civil
rights are not. For many of these people also, the threat of
nuclear war is real and urgent. The pattern is further com-

plicated by the exploitative role of Northern political and economic power (of the West and East) in the Southern hemisphere and third world. Much of the poverty and associated oppression in third world countries derives from the economic imperialism of the North and its political back-up. In peace and justice discussions the arms trade manipulated by the Western powers and the USSR for economic and political advantage and social survival gives an added cynical twist to the Western Christian's dilemma as peace-maker or justice-seeker.

In such a divided world a *Pax Christi* commitment to human rights indicates a willingness to confront seriously the disciples' dilemma. A theological reflection on that commitment may reveal the resources available to the Christian disciple in transforming the dilemma into genuine possibility.

Theological Difficulties

Recourse to theology never provides easy solutions to difficult problems. Theologians may often be accused of compounding rather than resolving the difficulties. Yet powerful causes, such as that of peace or human rights, when espoused by generous people may easily inhibit the kind of critical reason necessary to clear, coherent and fully effective support for the causes. In this discussion peace and human rights are historical, political causes. Although the debate continues under certain aspects, it will be assumed here that Christian and Church endorsement of these historical, political causes is an appropriate and required expression of Jesus' call to love of neighbour and to the development of his kingdom. Yet certain underlying doubts persist about the fittingness (*convenientia* as the Scholastics might say) of human rights language in Christian discourse and about the authenticity of peace language in any historical discourse.

Human rights language is a relatively recent addition to the moral and political vocabulary, and a still more recent addition to the vocabulary of Church and theology. Its gradual acceptance by Church and theology was based on the force of its moral insight and its political validity in protecting and promoting the dignity of the individual human being. This acceptance was not achieved without criticism and indeed resistance, which need not concern us here. The persisting doubts move along other lines.

The first and least troublesome concerns the individualism implied by certain uses of human rights language. The criticism powerfully enunciated by Marx in the middle of the nineteenth century has been largely met by the development of 'social and economic' rights which now constitute an integral part of the international code of human rights. The lingering suspicions rest on the Western emphasis on the individualist aspects, and the failure to develop parallel measures adequate to enforce social and economic rights, e.g. the right to work. A further and more difficult dimension of this individualism emerges in a discussion of the rights of peoples which are treated very restrictively and effectively reduced to aspects of individual rights by some international inhuman rights lawyers (e.g. Paul Sieghart, *The Lawful Rights of Mankind*, Oxford 1985).

A more serious difficulty in Christian reflection on human rights derives from the temptation, frequently yielded to, to translate all moral claims, indeed all morality, into rights language; this gives added force to the claim: 'My rights are being violated.' A particularly difficult example of this for Christian feminist disciples is the expression used in the abortion controversy, of 'a woman's right over her own body'. More generally, however, the attempt to translate all morality into the language of rights could constitute an enormous impoverishment of morality in the Christian — and in the wider human — tradition. Where would that leave friendship, perseverance, forgiveness, hope, humility, charity, courage, patience, prudence, joy, thanksgiving, mercy, compassion, love and all its associates? It is of course possible and proper to use critically, carefully and so, effectively, the language of human rights in appropriate moral, political and legal interests. But it is very tempting to go beyond that.

The deeper Christian suspicion of the language of right turns more immediately on the example and teaching of Jesus himself. How and when did he assert his rights? In the passion accounts which dominate the Gospel stories he never protests at the obvious injustice of false witnesses and biased judges or claims his clearly violated right to the Roman version of a fair trial. In the charter for disciples which Matthew's

Gospel presents in the Sermon on the Mount (Mt. 5, 6, 7), he seems to exclude very clearly for his disciples the personal claims which the tradition of human rights has developed and promoted. The blessed are often the meek, the merciful, the persecuted for righteousness' sake. A disciple struck on one cheek should turn the other. The call to love of enemies prepares for the climax of this section of the Sermon, to 'be perfect as your heavenly Father is perfect' (5:48).

The New Testament primacy of love to the point of laying down one's life for others, after the example of Jesus, seems scarcely compatible with the claims and assertiveness characteristic of the language of human rights. A more careful reading of the New Testament makes it clear that this way of surrender is not a way of individual perfection-seeking, which would indeed be self-centred, even masochistic, and so the very opposite of Christian loving. The surrender is to be for the sake of the others. In the context of Jesus' good news for the poor, liberation for the prisoners and healing for the sick (Lk. 4:18ff.), it could be argued that the disciples are called to sacrifice themselves for the sake of the deprived so that these may live more fully and with dignity. This will be at least partly realised in modern terms by respect for the relevant human rights.

Saying 'Peace, peace', when there is no peace. (Jer. 6:14)

The cry of Jeremiah over Jerusalem might be repeated in a thousand places today. Peace-talk can be easily misleading and inauthentic. Too often words like peace, forgiveness and reconciliation are invoked to secure the maintenance of an oppressive order rather than the achievement of true peace. The description of such an oppressive order as peace was exposed long ago by Tacitus: he has the Briton Calgacus address his troops on the meaning of the Pax Romana, 'Ubi solitudinem facuint, pacem appellant.' 'Where they make a desert, they call it peace' (Tacitus, *Agricola*, 30).

In South Africa as in so many other countries oppressors appeal (*appellant*) to the need to keep the peace, to promote reconciliation, without showing any sign of paying the cost of true peace. The cost must still be paid by the oppressed. It was against this false peace that Jeremiah directed his sharpest criticisms.

44

In a larger world context the Western and Northern concern for peace is seen very much as self-interest in an attempt to maintain the power and privilege of the wealthy and dominant. The current Western response to terrorism, when it is not utterly disproportionate and morally a form of terrorism itself, as in the attack on Libya, does not move much beyond the need for order — an order that serves Western interests. It ignores the absence of true peace for peoples subordinated to that order and those interests. Along the road of increased defence and anti-terrorist activity lie only very limited gains, even for the West, and very little true peace for anybody. Yet Christians retain their call to be peace-makers (Mt. 5:6). That peace has been bestowed by Jesus Christ (Jn. 14:27). It is characteristic of the Kingdom, the New Creation, the redeemed humanity which God inaugurated in Christ. Can such a Pax Christi have any real connection with the peace we have known as Pax Romana, Pax Anglicana, Pax Americana, Pax Sovietica? Is the imperial threat of all these inevitably desert-making? If so, what historical and political expression can Pax Christi ever achieve? Is it continually condemned to being merely eschatological, occurring only on the far side of history?

There are clear indications in Hebrew and Christian scriptures that the peace to be given by the God of Israel and of Jesus Christ has this worldly, historical and social implications. The very Hebrew greeting *Shalom*, used later by Jesus and Paul, connects with a very specific kingdom gift and condition. However a fuller response to disciples' difficulties about human rights and historical peace requires a more extended and positive theology of peace and justice, including human rights.

The Density and Dynamism of the Peace of Christ

Empty or oppressive orderliness does not reflect the biblical sense of peace. In the Hebrew tradition *shalom* signifies a rich reality of wholeness; well-being and flourishing which extends from the cosmos through society to God. It is a covenant reality, at once gift and task. The primary covenant gift of Godself ('I will be your God and you shall be my people' Lev. 26:12) provides the source and standard of all

45

the other covenant gifts of which peace and righteousness are outstanding and closely associated (Is. 32:16 f.; Ps. 72:3, 7; 85:10). The richness of the reality is not easily translatable into words available in the Greek or Latin tradition. The Septuagint Greek tradition of the Hebrew scriptures uses more than twenty terms to convey the range and richness of *shalom*. While *eirene* finally establishes itself, it must be stretched beyond its standard meaning of harmony and order. This difficulty is increased all the more into Latin, where *pax* has stronger overtones of legal order. The recovery of the density and dynamism of the Hebrew 'wholeness and flourishing', both economic and social, is essential to understanding the prophetic criticism and messianic promise of Jeremiah, Isaiah and Ezechiel. For Christians, criticism and promise are fulfilled in Jesus Christ.

The peace which Jesus gives (Jn. 14:27; 16:33), which Jesus is, is the peace of new Covenant and new Creation. The New (*Kaine*) Covenant (Testament) and Creation is salvation and reconciliation, healing of hostility and division, the opposites of peace. But it is not band-aid or superficial healing. It is not a cloaking of real and continuing divisions which could only be the pseudo-peace savaged by Jeremiah (6:14). It involves conversion, continuing conversion of the hostile to one another in Christ, in the human expression of their God (cf. Gal. 3:27 f.). And it opens the way to transformation and fulfilment for humanity and cosmos. What is achieved in Jesus is available now, operative now. It reaches out to further and final fulfilment. The density and dynamism of that achievement may be experienced as the gift of peace now and the call to build peace in hope for the future.

Orderly oppression and antagonistic individualism are equally opposed to the *Pax Christi* which brings the tradition and promise of *shalom* to completion. Peace is a living, developing reality in history, in community and in cosmos, far from the deadly desert of Tacitus' Britain.

Justice and the Respect for Difference

Righteousness or justice has a central role in the covenant relationship between Yahweh and Israel, which enters a new phase in the Christian covenant, 'It can be said without exaggeration that the Bible, taken as a whole, has one theme: The history of the revelation of God's righteousness' (H. H. Schrey). This righteousness, *sedaqah* is closely associated with *shalom*, (cf. Is. 32:16 etc.)

Sedaqah shares difficulties of translation with *shalom*. The Greek equivalent *dikaiosune* and the Latin *justitia* are more narrowly focused on the differentiation of people. Thomas Aquinas developed this idea under the rubric of *altereitas* or otherness. In the Hebrew tradition righteousness or justice, deriving from God and characteristic first of all of God in his covenant relationship, includes or at least overlaps with fidelity, mercy, kindness, love. The sharpness of opposition suggested by *altereitas* and developed in terms of *jus* or right, is not dominant. The one God who is the presence and power and claim of justice also embodies fidelity, mercy and loving-kindness. The plurality of gods for justice and peace and freedom in contemporary cultures undoubtedly sharpened the definition and differentiation of these basic words in ways foreign to the monotheistic Hebrew tradition.

Later philosophical and political developments associated with Locke, European enlightenment, the American and French revolutions sharpened these differences further. In the language of rights which moved from 'natural rights' through 'the rights of man' to the current phrase 'human rights', stark distinctions at once reinforced individuals and their claims. So they were protected under the law and against governments while running the risk of increasing isolation and fragmentation. Such a crude summary does scant justice to the developments of the last two hundred years in recognition, development and protection of individual human dignity through the medium of human rights.

Positively, human rights express the diversity of human beings, their relationships and structures. Negatively, they protect individuals from the abuses of power and government. Civil and political, social and economic rights as listed, for example, in the United Nations Declaration make positive claims to participation in the life and goods of society and the world as well as negative claims to immunity from interference by other individuals, groups and government. These claims are based on the dignity, uniqueness and inviolability of each human being. They are directed towards enabling the

47

individual to flourish, to realise her/his potential. In this way human rights are essential to the personal and social flourishing known to the Hebrew tradition as *shalom*. Rendering to each her/his due as envisaged in rights language and, more globally in Hebrew, as promoting *sedaqah*, righteousness or justice, provide the hard historical and political content of the condition of *shalom*. Of such peace Jeremiah dreamt when he called for true peace and condemned the false peace of an unjust, neglectful and exploitative society. The justice of Amos and the prophets, evidently absent in the neglect of the widow, the orphan and the stranger, expressed Yahweh's own bias towards the poor. Jesus' ministry to the excluded and the poor was the definitive expression of this divine bias.

The Kingdom which he prescribed and inaugurated as the social expression of the new Covenant is to ensure this protection and enablement of the weak within the community of friends (Jn. 15:15) and loving neighbours. This was the peace which Jesus bestowed and which, with grace (*charis*), constituted Paul's greeting of the Christian communities at Rome and Athens, Corinth, Galatia and Colossae as well as our liturgical greeting today.

Human Rights as Content and Pax Christ as Context

Justice, expressed in essential part by human rights, forms the hardcore of the peaceful community. Yet justice, and particularly its human rights dimension, relates more easily to differentiation with its tendency to divisions between persons and peoples, and to isolated individualism with its tendency to the fragmentation and atomisation of society and the world. Without bonding in communion, personal flourishing is not possible and personal rights are finally frustrated. In the sinful world, where the recognition of human rights is necessary to protect the individual against exploitation, powerful bonding forces are no less necessary to the flourishing in communion of persons. The salvation or healing which Jesus brought offers bonding force so that persons develop their full potential; they are saved and flourish in enriching communion with one another. The freedom and justice of the Kingdom which were later given secular expression in the liberty and equality of the eighteenth

48

century, leading in turn to the development of human rights, must be completed by fraternity and solidarity. In a sinful world fraternity requires forgiveness, repentance and reconciliation if it is to be achieved, sustained and renewed. The peace of Christ is a forgiving and reconciling peace as the New Testament frequently testifies. It includes the call and the grace to repent, to convert even if it means leaving one's gift at the altar and going first to be reconciled. The great secular triad liberty, equality and fraternity, recover their Jewish and Christian origins in Kingdom values of justice, freedom and peace. In that Kingdom the historical realities of human dignity, creativity and sinfulness find discernment, support and transformation through promotion of Human Rights under the banner of *Pax Christi.*

Rights, Peace and Christian Self-sacrifice

The peace of Christ, which is both divine gift and human call, finds its basic condition and hard content in the realisation of justice in society. Critical to that justice is the movement for human rights. Human rights activity as the protection of persons from oppression and exploitation and as the assurance of their participation in the God-given riches of cosmos and society, is a basic and continuing part of new creation, the new flourishing, the new *shalom*. The search for justice, and the struggle for rights will often encounter hostility and increase division. To prevent such division and hostility from finally frustrating the thrust of the human rights movement to human fulfilment and flourishing, the bonding, forgiving and reconciling powers of the peace of Christ will be required. *Pax Christi* provides the uniting power of communion to the necessarily differentiating power of human rights. Together they help forge some communal and personal expression of the Kingdom.

All this is achieved at cost to the promoters of the Kingdom. The Sermon on the Mount, the prophetic words of Jesus to his disciples about taking up one's cross, are reinforced by the prophetic critiques and images of Jesus' predecessors, such as Amos and Isaiah. They leave the disciples in no doubt that their peace-making and justice-seeking will demand drinking the chalice which he drinks. Where the justice-seeking takes the more particular form of promoting human rights the peace-making remains no less an imperative and the cost 'not less than everything' (T. S. Eliot).

6.

Creative Reconcilation

THE CALL to reconciliation in divisive societies frequently sounds like an endorsement of the oppressive *status quo*. Like so many rich human and Christian words, including peace, freedom and justice, reconciliation is used in a particular social context with particular presuppositions and interests which sometimes contradict its usage in a Gospel context. In this chapter, two aspects of the Christian usage of the word and idea are considered, one in general terms and the other in relation to a specific case.

The first usage is implicit in what has become an interesting discussion on 'the politics of forgiveness'. In these islands the discussion was initiated by Leeds theologian Haddon Wilmer. His concerns have been broadly European, indeed global, but much of the continuing debate has centred on Ireland and Anglo-Irish relations.

The second explicit usage addresses Jewish-Christian relations. As emerges in a number of chapters in this book, confronting the modern world in the late twentieth century demands a serious and repentant rethinking by Christians of their traditions of anti-Semitism and its contribution to the horrors of the Holocaust. Consideration of Jewish-Christian reconciliation should reveal the depths of the chaos, psychological, social and theological, in which we find ourselves and indicate the radical character of the new creation required of humanity and offered by God.

The general Christian understanding of and response to the problem of religion and politics must take account of the social context in which these occur and the social goal which they seek to promote. The social context of understanding and responding in this as in other areas operates ambiguously with creative and destructive potential. How to discern and distinguish these so that the creative potential may be realised as fully as possible and the destructive potential restricted as far as possible, is a difficult and delicate task. The hermeneutics of suspicion will alert one to the self-interest and distortion which the invocation of such a thoroughly Christian idea as forgiveness may involve. If it is not to issue in cynical paralysis it will need to be balanced by a hermeneutics of trust and emancipation.

The social goal of Christian faith is the coming of the Kingdom within history, if only partially and fitfully. In the continuing conflictive and sinful condition of history the anti-Kingdom lives and thrives. The political thrust of Christian faith is the overcoming of anti-Kingdom activities, relationships, structures and values, of sin and sinfulness, personal and social, through the saving power and presence of God in history which is called his reign or kingship or Kingdom. Forgiveness is a primary characteristic of the Kingdom announced and inaugurated by Jesus Christ. Historical political activity, relationships and structures must, in so far as they reflect that Kingdom, embody the value of forgiveness.

The (re)turn to society in theology involves a relationship between politics as reflecting in some sense and to some extent the inbreaking Kingdom and forgiveness as a historical feature of that Kingdom. Such theological language, however, requires very careful translation in any specific political context. Easy and uncritical movement between God's Kingdom and the political situation in the Middle East or Northern Ireland would obscure and compound the difficulties. This also applies to the Kingdom value of forgiveness. To abandon Kingdom power and values, including forgiveness, in the political sphere is, however, a betrayal of the hope that is in us as Christians and a denial of the saving presence of God through history, an implication, I believe, of Luther's Two Kingdoms Theology.

I. FORGIVENESS AND POLITICS

One significant feature of recent theology has been its concern with society and politics. European 'political theology',

Latin American 'liberation theology' and other third world theologies as well as feminist and black theologies all demonstrate theological preoccupation with social and political issues to the point where these issues influence and practically determine the matter and method of theology.

Churches and theologians have always been aware of the social significance of the Gospel. The social substance of the Kingdom preached and inaugurated by Jesus has never been simply ignored. At certain times it has been so strongly emphasised indeed that the partial historical and finally eschatological character of that Kingdom has been overlooked in reaching for a contemporary social embodiment of the Gospel message and Gospel grace. The thrust of Theodosian establishment influenced Christian thinkers and Church leaders down to our own time. In the aftermath of the Enlightenment and in reaction to the European wars of religion a 'privatisation' of Gospel and salvation (a rather different concept from the individualisation of certain Reformers) gradually separated the Gospel from social and political affairs. Politics and society in Europe and North America became increasingly secular, removed from the influence of Church and Gospel. And this became the new standard for the countries of Asia, Africa and Australasia. The process has not of course been completed. And new processes have begun with the fresh turn or return to society in Christian thinking and Church mission. This return is taking very different forms both in mission and theology. For many, such as the Moral Majority in the USA and other fundamentalist or conservative Christians, including some Roman Catholics, it is dominantly, if not exclusively, a seeking to restore traditional Church influence to traditional issues along largely traditional lines. For others, mainly the people influenced by the new political and liberation theologies, radical revision in the relationship of Church and theology with society and politics is envisaged.

These Christian developments of restoration or revision must also be considered in the global context of other major religions. Judaism, Islam, Hinduism and Buddhism; their self-understanding and consequent involvement in politics affect Christians very directly in areas where they are dominant and indirectly in terms of Christians' own understanding

53

of and response to the relations between religion and politics.

Before the political translation of Kingdom and forgiveness commences it is useful to look again at the historical operation of the Kingdom value of forgiveness in the area of personal relations. We believe we know what forgiveness means here and that it can actually operate effectively.

Forgiveness Between Persons

The Christian demand for forgiveness of the neighbour as enemy and assailant is based on the explicit teaching and example of Jesus (cf. Mt. 5:23-4, 43-5). Such human forgiveness is required as a condition for forgiveness of the human agent by God and is given climactic expression in Jesus' own final act of loving surrender on the Cross. It is not possible to accept Jesus in the Gospel accounts of him without recognising the summons to forgiveness. For some commentators this is the really distinctive characteristic of the morality taught and lived by Jesus, the morality of the Kingdom.

Forgiveness between human beings as a condition for and expression of forgiveness of human beings by the God of Jesus Christ derives its primary meaning from the biblical tradition and in particular from the Christian scriptures. Despite the emphasis on the interconnection between the operation of divine and human forgiveness, forgiveness in the biblical sense is gratuitous, offered freely and unconditionally by God and to be offered in the same way by human beings. The persistent loving initiatives of God in face of the human refusal and failure which are characteristic of the history of Israel reach a climax with the vineyard owner last of all sending his own son (Mk 12:1-9). The overall shape of Jewish and thus human history is formed by the gracious forgiving power of God overcoming human failure, alienation and division. The specification of the inbreaking Kingdom in and by Jesus defines more clearly the contours of this formative forgiveness.

With the gratuity of divine forgiveness and its human reflection comes its challenging and changing impact. Forgiveness moves to overcome alienation and division based on offence and rejection. It seeks to replace the hostile and hurtful with the accepting and enriching. The persons involved in the forgiving process are being invited and empowered to a new and transformed relationship. Forgiveness involves transformation of persons and relationships. Reconciliation provides another concept and image for the coming together of the previously hostile and divided.

The change, often described as conversion, which forgiveness as a completed process requires, implies repentance. Jesus' own announcement of the Kingdom (of forgiveness) included an immediate call to repentance. The initiative came from the forgiving God. That initiative carried its own loving healing power which could draw people out of their fearful and rejecting self-enclosure into the process of return to God. The liberating force of forgiveness genuinely available and seeking reconciliation is necessary to begin and sustain the process. Repentance is the appropriate and necessary response to that forgiving initiative.

It is a process involving two personal loving entities, divine with human or human with human. As one of the parties is human, the process is time-laden with all the variations of moods and moves which any human process requires. The words 'I forgive you' may play little or no role in that process just as the words 'Please forgive me' may never be voiced. The attitudes, activities and acceptance which these formulas of forgiveness and repentance express must however be present and communicated if the process is to be real. What is important for later consideration of 'Politics and Forgiveness' is the critical need for real communication of the forgiving process and the variety of forms which that communication may take. The forgiving father going out to meet his prodigal son expresses in so many ways beyond words an acceptance and forgiveness with which many of us can readily identify as father or son or both. The words 'I forgive you' spoken by the father might well have reduced the impact of the story and portrayed the father in a priggish light.

Inhibitions about the use of the formula, 'I forgive you', at least apart from the request 'Please forgive me', may be a healthy indication of everyone's need for forgiveness. Human reconciliation is always between sinners. Nobody can afford to play 'God almighty'. On the other hand the experience of being offended should, on the model of the gospels, lead one to seek out the offender and to propose reconciliation without waiting for the offender to make the first move. The dynamics of Christian forgiveness require that initiative although the statics of human failure may frustrate it. Mutual acceptance in love by offended and offender completes the process of forgiveness and repentance. Expressions may vary enormously provided they are mutually intelligible, drawing both parties more consciously into reconciling love.

Such reconciliation occurs within a continuing sinful world in which it may be the source of fresh offence and division. The prodigal's elder brother alienated by the father's forgiving reception and celebration, is as typical as the forgiving father. Forgiveness and reconciliation seek to enlarge the community of loving acceptance. Sometimes they disrupt and divide it in a new way. The politics of forgiveness even on the domestic scale has to take account of this potential for offence and seek to prevent its realisation.

The offence to the elder brother suggests another difficulty in the forgiveness process. The father saw himself as acting on behalf of the family and called for a family celebration. The elder brother did not see himself as bound by that representation. Again he is not peculiar in this. Forgiveness by representative even on the family level is difficult in theory and in practice. The forgiving voices of particular family members faced with the killing of one of their own is properly impressive. It rekindles faith in the loving possibilities of human beings. It may not speak for all the bereaved. And it may not presume to speak for the actual victim. Representative forgiveness in that sense is hardly meaningful. For the offence which the bereaved suffered, and it can be enormous, they can be forgiving and seek to take the whole family with them. Such forgiving may and should lead the killers to repentance. The bereaved cannot give the killers direct forgiveness, nor can the latter, after the victim's death, receive it.

Yet within the Christian tradition belief in a deeper forgiveness has always prevailed. Homicide was one of those serious crimes for which the early Christian community explicitly offered forgiveness by reintegration, after a period of repentance, into the community of the saints. Such forgiving power, mediated through the believing community, derived from the Kingdom power of forgiveness, was passed

on through Jesus to the community of disciples. God's acceptance of the sinner in Jesus and then in the community of
disciples transcended the limitations of all human forgiveness.
But how? Theologians have not sufficiently wrestled with
this. Can God from on high as it were forgive the murderer
on behalf of the victim? What kind of involvement with the
victims by God does this suggest? What kind of God does
it suggest? The possibility and reality of forgiveness, a central
characteristic of the Judaeo-Christian tradition, may have
much more to offer on the existence and nature of God than
theologians have hitherto investigated.

Political Forgiveness

Hostility and destructive divisions are at least as common in
political relationships within and between states as they are
in personal relationships. They are equally counter-Kingdom
and just as much in need of transforming forgiveness. The
statement of need is almost the only simple statement that
can be made about forgiveness in political relationships. The
roots of political divisions are so tangled and their historical
genesis so gradual that original offended and offender may
have long disappeared although the unforgiven consequences
persist. The difficulties and ambiguities already noted in the
discussion of personal forgiveness are considerably increased
and compounded in the search for political forgiveness. Given
the undoubted Christian call and human need for such forgiveness in the political struggles for co-existence, mutual
acceptance and enrichment, more reflection on the meaning
and method is urgently required. The unsystematic and incomplete reflections offered here are inspired by the work of
Gandhi and such successors as Martin Luther King. Here we
see a serious practical attempt to relate the vision and values
of the Sermon on the Mount, the charter of the Kingdom, to
urgent and apparently intractable political problems. In what
follows I will not be following either Gandhi or King literally
but offering my own synthesis based on their work.

It is not of course possible to describe Gandhi as a Christian
believer or to see Jesus or the Sermon on the Mount as the
exclusive or even primary influence on his thought and work.
They were important influences. For Martin Luther King

57

they were of course much more important.

It is not necessary to claim complete success for either Gandhi or King. Yet if humankind is to survive its present combination of crises involving the threat of nuclear war between the super-powers of East and West and the threat of multiple wars between privileged and deprived, more approximately ascribed to North and South, it will need an alternative to the culture of war still dominant with the powerful and powerless. The best hopes of an alternative rest with the tradition of Gandhi and Luther King. This tradition can claim powerful antecedents in the New Testament and the early centuries of the Church. Despite the dominance of the just war tradition in Christianity for 1,500 years, the anti-war, peace-making (paci-fist) alternative survived, if very tenuously at times.

The question of how far a war-culture is compatible with forgiveness in politics demands fuller analysis and I will return to it later. My more immediate concern is how far the ideas and practices of Gandhi and others illuminate the meaning and possibility of political forgiveness in situations of oppression, estrangement and open hostilities.

Gandhi and King did not in any way seek to obscure the existence of oppression and its destructive consequences. They were equally clear about the distinction between the oppressor and the oppressed. They were committed to overcoming the oppression and saw that this involved a transformation of attitudes, relationships and structures in which the powerless and oppressed would be on equal terms with the powerful. In the achievement of transformation the oppressed or powerless would be the immediate engine of change.

In all this they did not differ much from many other revolutionaries in human history. Their most obvious difference from others lay in their choice of methods, non-violent methods as they are inadequately called. Their deeper differences, particularly in the case of Gandhi, lay in understanding the relationship between means and ends and more deeply still in the analysis of oppressive structures and their correlative transformation.

In recognising the means of political change as inextricably linked to the results, Gandhi excluded any means finally destructive of human beings. To adopt destructive means would be to include destruction and its possibility as part of the new political order. This would be to deface the vision and defeat the purpose of the liberation movement. Clearly a movement which refuses counter-destructiveness in face of destructive oppression has important possibilities for love of enemies and political forgiveness.

These possibilities are confirmed in a vision of the mutual enslavement of oppressor and oppressed and their need for mutual emancipation. There are indications that Gandhi saw the British as entrapped by their imperial power, role and structures. This did not cloud his view of British responsibility for the past or their obligations to the present and future. Their entrapment and consequent blindness (a frequent combination) made it imperative for the Indian people and their leaders to seek their own emancipation but as a way of emancipation for the British also. This of course required protest, resistance and pressure of a rich variety but it precluded elimination. To eliminate the British and their supporters in the struggle for independence would be to deny their emancipation. It would exclude the liberated structures and relationships of acceptance and equality in which the British and Indian peoples should eventually participate. These transformed structures of liberation, acceptance and equality would be a powerful political expression of forgiveness and repentance.

To appreciate the fuller thrust of this analysis and practice it is worth comparing it with that other great twentieth-century 'philosopher' of anti-colonial radical social change, Frantz Fanon. For him the only way of emancipation for the native oppressed lay in the elimination of settler-oppressor. In him the war-culture in its revolutionary mode reached towards a mysticism of destruction. With him forgiveness in politics is not so much irrelevant or impossible as counter-revolutionary, counter-political.

All this leaves us with serious questions about the compatibility of the war-culture with forgiveness in politics. At one level the search for political forgiveness from behind the parapets offers little prospect of the transformation of relationships. More seriously it may be interpreted as — and it may well be — a manipulation by the powerful of the powerless, by the oppressor of the oppressed. At a different level it may be a well-intentioned but fundamentally misguided way of trying to combine two irreconcilable forms of politics, much too crudely summarised in the words, 'If you don't forgive me I will beat you into the ground.' Some of the 'reconciliation' in Europe after World War II was born of shame and horror at the previous decades but more of it was a laying aside of some traditional hostilities in face of more immediate and greater threats. It is doubtful whether reconciliation in our politics without the pressure of a common fear is possible.

Perhaps in politics as elsewhere fear could prove the beginning of wisdom. And the limited reconciliation born in fear could provide a useful starting point for a larger process. But if that process is to be one of forgiveness in any Kingdom sense or indeed in any sense that is humanly significant, it will have to include a gradual shift from a war-culture, and a progressive transformation of relationships between powerful and powerless.

II. JEWISH-CHRISTIAN RECONCILIATION

A small country such as Ireland with a very small Jewish population might seem an unlikely meeting place for the theme of Jewish-Christian reconciliation particularly when it has such an enormous problem of Christian-Christian reconciliation. Indeed the theme Reconciliation might seem particularly inappropriate anywhere in the world at this time — with divisions and hostilities, wars and terrorism expanding or impending. From Northern Ireland through the Middle East to Sri Lanka, the Philippines, Southern Africa, South and Central America, not only the absence of reconciliation but the apparent impossibility of it suggest that the theme is much too grand, not just for Ireland but for the world, not just for Jews and Christians but for humankind. And where it apparently exists it may well be the fruit and guarantee of oppression, gross and political as in so much of Eastern Europe or subtle, and economic, racist or sexist as in so much of the rest of the world. If reconciliation is the overcoming of hostile divisions such as the obviously racial ones in South Africa, it can be too easily invoked to protect

60

the power of the privileged and to make the deprived pay the further price of assuaging the guilt of the privileged at no real cost to them.

The recent debate on forgiveness and the Holocaust revealed some of that difficulty. A chorus of Christian voices, symbolised by President Reagan's visit to Bitberg, called for forgiveness by the Jews for the horrors of Auschwitz and the rest. Many Jews had genuine and proper difficulties about how anybody could forgive on behalf of the six million who had perished. Some were more properly suspicious that this kind of forgiving would be linked inextricably with forgetting while some of the argument suggested a new burden for the surviving and continuing Jewish people. They had refused forgiveness to the Nazi oppressors, thereby failing to follow the example of Jesus and his Christian followers. There are difficult theological, psychological and sociological problems here. In their hectoring and unrepentant tones, some Christian calls to Jews for forgiveness of the Holocaust can sound impertinent and appallingly insensitive. Yet they must be made.

The great dimensions of reconciliation are cause for humility at the outset of our discussions. For Christians the sweep of the Pauline vision of reconciliation of all peoples in Christ (cf. II Cor. 5 etc.), may lead them to take the word for the deed, the 'indicative' of divine grace suppressing the 'imperative' of human task. The peculiar Jewish-Christian asymmetry and alienation render the application of such texts particularly difficult in Jewish-Christian dialogue, where the figure of Jesus and certainly his historical understanding in Christology is at the root of our separation. A further refinement of this difficulty emerges with the efforts of some Christians to interpret the Holocaust in the light of Calvary. Progress is possible, I believe, towards reconciliation between Jews and Christians and by Jews and Christians in the larger world which draws on their proper religious resources, including Christian understanding of Calvary and Jewish understanding of the Holocaust. But the steps will be slow and delicate and involve much painful retracing of past tramping over people's graves, too much of it in jack-boots.

In the Christian scriptures the word used for reconciliation is *katallassein* (or *diallassein*) which derives from the word 'other' (*allos*) and is related to overcoming hostile otherness or estrangement. Reconciliation can only operate to over-come the estrangement if it takes the others, the strangers, seriously. In philosophy and literature, contemporary and ancient, as in the religious traditions of Israel and Christianity, the other is critical to human understanding and human living. Each human other in her or his otherness and strangeness is at once gift and threat to us. So much of human and biblical history reflects this ambiguity in our relations to one another. As individuals and as groups we confront one another as potentially enriching and potentially destructive. As Jews and Christians, as male and female, as black and white, in our strangeness or otherness we can inspire fear which may turn to hostility and destruction or we can evoke recognition and eventually love of the gift we may be to one another.

The Genesis account of the creation and fall of Adam and Eve follows the gift and threat pattern as Adam hymns his new-given wife only to react accusingly later: 'She did it. She gave me to eat.' More deeply for Israel the gift relation-ship which characterised creator and creation, particularly human creation, rapidly turned to threat with human failure to respect the divine conditions. And this is to characterise for Israel the history of humanity and of Israel itself. The divine other, whose self-giving to humanity spans creation and covenant, becomes inevitably judging and threatening to a refusing, rejecting and so alienated humanity.

To confirm and deepen this reading of divine-human relations we recall the outstanding characteristic of God as the holy one, the holy one of Israel. This is an expression of the transcendence of God whose recognition was a particular achievement of the faith of Israel. Holy translates *qadosh* which in origin meant the separated one, the other. It was ultimate otherness of the transcendent God of Israel which made him the inexhaustible source of loving creativity which human weakness could not always tolerate and so rendered judging and threatening. The ultimate other, the holy one, *tremendum et fascinans*, awe-inspiring (fearful) and fascin-ating (attractive) was explored by Rudolf Otto in ways which generally reflect the tradition of Israel and the par-ticular feature of it developed here. Without pursuing for the moment the more detailed history of Israel or Christianity, what is relevant is the continuing ambiguity of the other, as individual or group. In critical cases the threatening element becomes so overwhelming and the other becomes an unmitigated source of evil, is demonised. How this can happen in racial, national and sexual relations is part of our continuing experience. That it should happen in religious relations involves a particular infidelity to their common fathers in Abraham, Moses and the prophets and equivalent blasphemy of their common God. Yet the history of anti-semitism reveals in many periods a demonisation of Jews from the consequences of which popes occasionally had to protect them. The demonisation reached its completion with Nazism, and the protection proved tragically inadequate. The elimination of the demon Jewish people in genocide, the most appalling crime in human history, was to be the final solution to the threatening, intolerable others.

People engaged in Jewish-Christian dialogue could not be accused of ignoring the Holocaust. Even for them appreciation of the depth and range of the horror comes slowly and fitfully. For many other Christians it is just one more horror. We have a surfeit of horrors and to remain sane we must not dwell on too many or on any for too long. Yet without a wounding sense of the Holocaust Christians cannot hope to understand their Jewish friends and neighbours. Without a regular return by Church leaders and theologians to the revelation of human and Christian sinfulness which Auschwitz and Belsen and all the others provide, there is no hope of understanding the Jewish others and the Christian threatening, sometimes demonic role in their history. The depths of our alienation, the challenge of our reconciliation, is how far we have demonised one another. For Christians the Holocaust is the essential revelation of all that.

In speaking of reconciliation we have much to be modest, indeed humble, about. Mutual toleration is not so stable and secure that we can easily bypass it. It will always be a task which may never be taken for granted. In so many relationships, personal and social, secular and religious, apparent and easy toleration suddenly breaks down. This can happen in marriage, between friends and colleagues, as it can happen between religious, racial and national groups. Jews and blacks and other 'strangers' in Europe have good reason to be wary of sudden outbursts of intolerance as their otherness is perceived as threatening and is threatened in turn. Coexistence, with adequate structures to ensure continuing toleration particularly of the traditionally persecuted, is an essential minimum in all our societies. I emphasise the traditionally persecuted because the malevolent forces of history do not quickly disappear; they still influence us all. Remembering the Holocaust is not a safeguard for Jews only but also for us with our destructive heritage.

Mutual toleration is not enough — even to ensure mutual toleration. We have to aim higher with all the humility the revelation of Auschwitz induces. Coexistence is meaningless without collaboration — working together for a world in which destructive alienations are confronted and gradually overcome. To settle for toleration without seeking for further reconciliation would be no more than a caging of the beast. This may be sometimes the best available but it is not a good way of human relating or indeed any guarantee of mutual acceptance.

Yet the range and depth of alienation suggest an impossible task. Building our fortresses, our cages, higher seems the only realistic policy. 'Soccer thugs' are the new paradigm of alienated, threatening destructive humanity. For Jews and Christians this won't do. With their sense of the human other as created in the image of the divine other and so enjoying creative, enriching potential for all, the call to realising that creative, enriching potential is inescapable. And the empowerment, the divine empowering presence comes with the call. In neither of our traditions is there law without grace. The power and call we share are directed to the vision we share in the final kingship of peace and justice and love.

And in so many situations it is possible to have an understanding of the problem and a vision of its solution without knowing how to get from one to the other. Here I can offer only one limited reflection on the task of reconciliation as a shared responsibility of Jews and Christians.

Recognising the enormous, if ambiguous, contribution both Jew and Christians have made to moral understanding and moral practice in the world, I hope it will not be too strange, too other, to invoke as source of understanding and practice here, a man from outside both these traditions, the

64

Mahatma Gandhi. He is I believe the moral genius of this century and perhaps of many centuries. I can only briefly advert to some of his ideas and practices here. He faced very serious situations of alienation in South Africa and his native India. In struggling with them he developed a philosophy and a strategy which is sometimes very inadequately summarised under the heading of 'non-violence'. This carried no implication for him of passivity in the face of evil and oppression or of inability to recognise and oppose the oppressors. One of his great insights was into the potential gift character of the oppressors as well as of the oppressed, their capacity for mutual enrichment and his awareness of the enslavement of the oppressors as well as of the oppressed. The British in India were also in need of emancipation, although their enslavement was a considerably more comfortable, 'gin and tonic' type. To do justice to both sides and to achieve justice Gandhi ruled out killing, which would eliminate rather than emancipate the British and for the surviving Indians would impoverish their humanity, their otherness. The goal of a new human community must be integral to the means used. The political success of Gandhi was mixed — like that of most revolutionaries, including armed revolutionaries. The applicability of philosophy and strategy may not be easily assumed. Buber had some serious questions for him about Jewish resistance under the Nazis. For all that I do not see any alternative in a responsible campaign by Jews and Christians for reconciliation in the world, which does not take the hostile others seriously as potentially enriching others and gradually replace the strategies and indeed culture of war with the strategies and culture of reconciling human others through mutual recognition, respect and emancipation. The final achievement of all that belongs to the Kingdom which lies ahead of history. The divine power and call of our common God is to seek its partial realisation even now.

7.

The Challenge of the Holocaust

IN UNDERTAKING to discuss the Holocaust at all, a Christian, and particularly a European Christian of a certain age, may seem to be acting presumptuously. As an outsider and perhaps a guilty outsider or bystander, he or she is exposed to the danger of gross insensitivity to, and misunderstanding of, one of the most intense and extensive events of suffering in human history. At the same time one is subject to the pressure of minimising and rationalising European Christian involvement and responsibility for what some Christian theologians have called the most significant Church event of the century.

How can an outsider to the victims, like myself, hope to understand what they suffered and what their survivors and successors still suffer? How can an insider of the European Christian community hope to confront honestly the failures, the complicity, the active engagement and even endorsement by so many from his own community?

For myself I regard this attempt to understand and confront as a permanent part of my Christian life and theology — or reflexion on Christian life. It is my hope that I can contribute to making that task of understanding and confronting a permanent and effective part of the Christian lives and reflexion of as many Christians as possible.

The Moral Challenge

I take my challenge, or my discussion of the challenge in two stages — what I call the moral challenge and the theological challenge. The moral challenge I see as, above all, a challenge of remembering.

In a world beset by countless atrocities, from rape in the next street, to torture in the next country, and the starvation of millions in the next continent, it might seem arrogant of Jews, and eccentric of certain Christians, to insist on remembering the Holocaust. Indeed the legitimate Jewish preoccupation with the prevention of recurrence — *ni veda* (never again) as inscribed at Dachau — seems to many contemporaries relatively insignificant in the face of the more immediate threat of nuclear annihilation of all humanity.

In the fire storms of total or even restricted nuclear war, the Nazi gas chambers might appear no more than local forest fires, the six million Jews eclipsed by the incalculable hundreds of millions of the nuclear holocaust.

At a more personal level people ask, why can't the Jews forgive and forget? Remembering must keep alive bitterness and division. It may even prevent Jews and particularly Jews in Israel from dealing with the very real problems of living in peace with their Palestinian and other Arab neighbours.

These difficulties can and should be answered in various ways by all human beings, because the holocaust is a moral challenge to more than Christians, and indeed to more than Europeans.

For Christians there will be a particular dimension to the answers which their own faith requires. However, to hope for any answers at all we must begin by remembering, by recalling the destructive and distinctively destructive enterprise which was central to the Nazi programme under Hitler in Germany from 1933 to 1945.

Hitler, with his anti-Jewish programme, did not appear from nowhere to become Chancellor of Germany in 1933. The previous ten years had prepared his way to power *and* to the implementation of his anti-Jewish plans. It might have prepared or at least forewarned his fellow countrymen in politics and in the Churches, but his anti-Jewish attitudes may have found too many reinforcing resonances among too many people for them to look closely at, or resist, his plans.

In his Table Talk he recalls his reply to two protesting bishops: 'I am only implementing what you have been preaching for 2,000 years.'

Christian remembering will have to go much further back than 1945 or 1933 if it is to confront Christian involvement and responsibilities. However, remembering the holocaust itself is our immediate concern.

The phenomenon has been extensively documented and the crude figures are widely known — about 6 million Jews, including one million children, perished in the extermination camps, in transit to them, in the labour camps and elsewhere.

The sufferings behind the figures, the degradation and torture involved for the victims, the day-by-day living, or rather dying, which these millions of innocent victims endured, are preserved for us in some remarkable accounts by victims, accounts which survived in extraordinary ways, as well as the testimony of survivors themselves. To remember, in the moral sense required here, we need some informed awareness of the range of horror in number and kind of victims, as detailed in the many excellent histories; but we perhaps need even more to share the sense of intense suffering conveyed by the witness of the victims and the survivors. To be exposed to the range and depth of the Holocaust as experienced by European Jews in those years is the first step in Christian response.

Other people, as well as Jews, have been subjected to destructive programmes of great range and intensity, such range that they themselves have been labelled genocidal — the Turkish massacre of the Armenians in the years 1915-16 is the most notable example in this century, although the fate of indigenous people in Latin and North America may also be cited, among many others.

Without getting ourselves involved in a comparative study of horrors I find myself in agreement with American scholar Stephen Katz on the distinctiveness of the Jewish holocaust, based on its clearly formulated intention of exterminating all Jews *as Jews*, and not as political or economic or religious opponents. Biology rules OK.

Conversion, assimilation or emigration would no longer suffice. The horror moves from the victims and the oppressed to the oppressor, whose vision of humanity demands the extermination of this particular people. Raoul Hillberg in his classic history *The Destruction of the European Jews* has shown that the extermination was not the result of war pressure or mob rule but a carefully planned, highly organised and brilliantly executed programme, operated with machine-like efficiency.

68

This involved the co-operation of people across the spectrum of society in Germany and in the occupied countries, from transport workers to registrars of births, including Church registrars; judges and endless minor and major bureaucrats. It was not just the SS and camp guards, the butchers of Belsen, but private and public workers at all levels of society contributed to this successful, perhaps most successful, bureaucratic operation involving, as Hillberg points out, first of all the whole process of identifying the Jews, then of expropriating them, then of concentrating them and finally of exterminating them.

And of course beyond Germany and the occupied countries, the rejection of emigrants and the refusal, for example, to bomb the railway lines to the camps, showed the Allies largely indifferent to the continuance of the Holocaust. The phenomenon requires much fuller and more refined consideration. As a deliberate plan to exterminate people with all the assistance of modern technology in the heart of civilised Europe in the twentieth century, it calls in question all the grand claims of European civilisation and twentieth-century progress.

Many commentators, like Uri Tal, have properly and effectively examined the Holocaust as a judgment on that civilisation and progress. They see it in particular as a crucial illustration of human beings seeking to play God, making decisions not only on who should live and who should die, but on the very self-definition of the human — the human superman — from which the lesser breeds, and pre-eminently the Jews, must be excluded and so exterminated.

There is much to this argument which connects in turn with the promethean arrogance that may unleash a nuclear holocaust. There are important implications for future human survival in our memories of the Jewish Holocaust, in the temptation to play God, so magnified by modern technological achievement, and in the European sense of autonomy. Only a humble sense of interdependence among all human beings and of human limitation, founded ultimately in the creaturely condition of humanity, will secure us against possible self-destruction by design or by accident, but always by arrogance. Remembering the Holocaust of the Jews is integral to preventing the holocaust of humanity.

The designed destruction of a people presents problems for our belief in humanity. It presents equally serious problems for belief in God, particularly where the people destroyed and the people destroying are both peoples of God, and of the same God. The temptation for Christians to attribute the Holocaust simply to the godless arrogance of a godless people must be resisted. The involvement of Christians, and the influence of historic Christian attitudes to the Jews, were too obvious and too effective.

A further dimension of the moral challenge to Christians is to recognise the extent of Christian involvement and the influence of traditional Christian anti-Semitism. Even if Hitler was invoking a self-serving argument in his reply to the bishops, he was also shrewdly exploiting a traditional Christian weakness. From New Testament times, through the medieval into the modern era, Jews had been treated harshly by Christians, as somehow accursed by God, above all for their rejection of Jesus and their part in his death. The remembering to which the Holcaust summons Christians does not allow them to ignore pre-Holocaust anti-Semitism, and its long ugly history, or indeed the possible or actual survival of that in the post-Holocaust world.

The hatred, it was frequently hatred, and the injustice, it was always injustice, which preceded and influenced the Holocaust, must be confronted by Christians that they may be exorcised and overcome. For the sake of Christian fidelity itself, for the sake of Christian morality, remembering the Holocaust and its antecedents is essential.

The Theological Challenge

In this, the second stage of my argument, I take up what I call the theological, as opposed to the moral, challenge, and I take it up for the most part in terms that take me back to an understanding of Christianity and of Judaism that, borrowing perhaps the Vatican II's phrase about 'reading the signs of the times', might be more deeply understood as the revelation out of darkness.

The Holocaust was darkness, one of the darkest episodes in human history. Language breaks down when you begin to invoke particular nouns and adjectives in regard to the

the Holocaust. But what did that darkness do to us? It put at stake first of all the people of Israel. It clearly put them at stake as an actual historical people. The Nazi programme was directed against the people who by blood were Jews. The success of the programme would be achieved only when the last Jew who could be counted by blood had been exterminated. So clearly the people was at risk in its very existence.

The question that raises for our belief in humanity I have already touched on. It has been taken up in terms of the criticism of the godless, or would be god-like, arrogant aping of God, to which modern man may be tempted. But what it meant for Jews in their relation to God, as a theological challenge, was of course much more immediate, direct and devastating.

Could the God who had called them, with whom they had a covenant, allow them to lapse out of existence? Physical disappearance of the Jews was part of the plan, the intentionality that we have mentioned earlier, and it must create enormous problems for our belief in a God who cares; and for Jewish belief in a God who is covenanted. It is the survivors who raise the second half of the question: can they survive as a covenanted people any more?

Somebody as penetrating, and as logical and as lucid in his argument as Richard Rubenstein thinks not, because the God, in so far as he was a God of the covenant and the covenanted people, has failed his people. He is no longer worthy of their allegiance, given what they had to endure, what they had to suffer. In so far as he ever existed, he no longer commands Jewish allegiance. This is one kind of argument put forward by some very influential post-Holocaust Jewish thinkers. It is not by any means the only kind of argument. There is a considerable body of Jewish thought which confronts the Holocaust head on, and in various ways offers us lines on how God remained faithful and the people must remain faithful, but it is not easy to understand or accept these lines of argument.

There is another element to the whole question which for Christians is particularly difficult. I have touched on it already in terms of the moral challenge and the moral responsibility: how can the Christian people survive the Holocaust? How can they survive as credible witnesses to the God of love, to the

God of history, to the God of creation and power? How can they offer themselves to the world as witnesses to that God, when the history of their anti-Semitism, and the involvement or indifference of so many of their members, allowed this horrifying episode to happen.

There are then three great theological questions or challenges which confront us as we tackle the Holocaust, the challenges of the existence of Israel, the existence of a credible Christian community, the existence of God.

So we work our way back to what in the end is the most important question of all, the question of God. One couldn't, as it were, in the face of the darkness, rehabilitate simply and easily the Christian and Jewish tradition of God as all-loving and all-powerful. But one can get hints. One can get perhaps enough hints to go on. One can get at least signs of hope.

Many of these signs of hope, of course, come for us first of all from the Jewish people themselves, from within the camps. If we are to pray after the Holocaust, it's partly because people could still pray in Auschwitz and Belsen. If we are to have some hope for humanity after the Holocaust, it's partly because there were people of hope in the camps. If we are to address God and hold on to God, it is because, at least in part, there were people in the camps who held on to God.

But that obviously would not be entirely satisfactory. Of course people who pray, people who witness by their lives and their heroism, are in so many ways the signs of God, the sacraments of God's presence. But yet, people might be deluded, people might keep themselves going by self-deception. We have at least to consider that. We have to consider the genuine problems that arise, the problems that seem to me to be taken up so marvellously in Elie Wiesel's book so aptly called *Night*.

François Mauriac, who wrote the introduction to this book when it was first published, noted how a child lost his faith when confronted with absolute evil. Wiesel's account is as follows:

Never shall I forget that night, the first night in camp, that has turned my life into one long night seven times cursed and seven times sealed. Never shall I forget that smoke. Never shall I forget the little faces of the children whose bodies I saw turned into wreaths of smoke beneath the silent blue sky. Never shall I forget those flames which consumed my faith forever. Never shall I forget that nocturnal silence which deprived me for all eternity of the desire to live. Never shall I forget those moments which murdered my God, and my soul, and turned my dreams to dust. Never shall I forget these things, even if I am condemned to live as long as God himself. Never.

It's that sense of the night, of the darkness that had to be confronted, that was confronted, that we ourselves have still to wrestle with. It raises problems for our view of a loving and powerful God taking care of his own. What kind of God was left to the people in the camps?

Another passage, a very famous passage from Wiesel, will help us I think:

One day when we came back from work we saw three gallows rearing up in the assembly place, three black crows. Roll call. SS all around us. Machine guns raised. The traditional ceremony. Three victims in chains, and one of them the little servant, the little Dutch boy, the sad-eyed angel. The SS seemed more preoccupied, more disturbed than usual. To hang a young boy in front of thousands of spectators was no light matter. The head of the camp read the verdict. All eyes were on the child. He was lividly pale, almost calm, biting his lips. The gallows threw its shadow over him.

This time the lager kapo refused to act as executioner. Three SS replaced him. The three victims mounted together onto the gallows. The three necks were placed at the same moment within the nooses.

'Long live liberty!' cried the two adults, but the child was silent.

'Where is God? Where is he?' someone behind me asked.

At a sign from the head of the camp the three chairs tipped over. Total silence throughout the camp. On the horizon the sun was setting.

'Bare your heads!' yelled the head of the camp. His voice was raucous. We were weeping. 'Cover your heads!'

Then the march past began. The two adults were no

longer alive. Their tongues hung swollen, blue-tinged, but the third rope was still moving. Being so light the child was still alive. For more than half-an-hour he stayed there, struggling between life and death, dying in slow agony under our eyes and we had to look him full in the face. He was still alive when I passed in front of him. His tongue was still red, his eyes not yet glazed. Behind me I heard the same man asking, 'Where is God now?' And I heard a voice within me answer him, 'Where is he? Here he is. He is hanging there on this gallows.' That night the soup tasted of corpses.

It's somewhere there in the heart of the darkness that we discover the God of Israel and the God of Jesus. It's somewhere there, taking on man's evil, suffering with the victims of man's inhumanity to man, that our God is to be found. This is part of Jewish tradition as it is part of Christian. I don't want to make any easy and quick moves from the suffering Servant of Israel to Auschwitz, or from Calvary to Auschwitz, but I believe that in both traditions we have something of that sense of a God who is at the heart of creation, at the heart of history rather than simply Lord of it. In dealing with the problem of evil in general and then the intensification of that problem with which the Holocaust presents us, we have many responses, but one of them of course, and a central one, is that if God is to respect human freedom then he must tolerate evil.

In the face of Auschwitz it can seem a very heartless position for God. But if God who creates and gives humanity freedom, thereby accepting that humanity will do evil, if he (or she, there are no pronouns appropriate to God) is with the victims of that evil, enduring that evil also, the perspective shifts. But is it possible for Christians or Jews to recognise the awesome, transcendent God as genuinely compassionate, co-suffering with the human victims in history? After the Holocaust and with the biblical accounts of Israel and Jesus, we seem driven to accept God's identification with his suffering people, a truly suffering God who endures the destruction of man-made chaos as a way to new creation.

If we are not able to find God on the gallows we cannot find him in the sky. If we are not able to find God in the 'absent from history' then we may not hope to find him in the triumphs and fulfilments of history.

It remains a struggle to believe that in and through the Holocaust, the God who created us, who covenanted us, as Jews and Christians, was himself (or herself) enduring and suffering, and thereby ensuring hope, ensuring faith, ensuring love. This is the God who is revealed to us out of the darkness.

In a different way one might think of God's infinite capacity as a capacity to take on all the sufferings of the others. And this takes me to the last point I want to make, that it is God taking on the suffering, being involved in the suffering, who is summoning Christians. We have somehow, after two thousand years of anti-Semitism and above all after the Holocaust, to allow ourselves to be inhabited by Jewish suffering. That will be the source of our finding anew our common God. It will be the source of our conversion. It will be our final response to the challenge of the Holocaust. Inhabited by the sufferings of the Jewish people, we must recognise more fully and more faithfully our common God, and let that recognition be released in all that we are and do. A significant liberation of Christians must come through their acceptance of their responsibility in regard to Jews; through their entry into what Jews have suffered, and their recognition with Jews, of the God, the shared God, who takes them beyond that suffering. As Paul anticipated we may, then, Jews and Christians, finally share in the new creation.

8.

Sacraments and Society

THE SECOND Vatican Council was at once a climax and summary of theological and pastoral developments within the Roman Catholic Church and a starting-point and resource-centre for new developments. Many Roman Catholics are still unable or unwilling to share in the climactic developments which occurred at Vatican II. Many others have progressed so far beyond it even as starting-point that they are out of touch, if not out of sight, of those still to reach the goals of the Council. Other Christian Churches with and without the influence of Vatican II, are experiencing the same tensions. Vatican II itself, providentially or accidentally, provided at its beginning and end clear indications of the boundaries of Christian existence. Its first document dealt with the liturgy, its last with the Church in the modern world. Certainly participation in the liturgy is, for Catholics, a critical mark of belonging to their community. All Churches, like all human beings, have to live in the modern world. Their common involvement in liturgy and world constitutes a challenge to the most diverging Catholics and Christians. I wish to explore one typically Catholic dimension of this under the rubric of sacraments and society, terms that are more restricted and maybe more precise than liturgy and world.

Theology and Society

The developments in Roman Catholic theology which culminated in the constitution on the Church in the Modern World (*Gaudium et Spes*) provided a critical integration of the liberal contribution to society over the previous century. This was reflected in the optimistic tone of the document and more significantly in the emphasis on the individual person's dignity and value. The social dimension of the person and the social forces which enter into the very formation of person received much less attention. In the late 1960s social dimension and social forces became much more the concern of Catholic theologians both in Europe and in the first world with 'Political Theology', and in Latin America and the third world with 'Liberation Theology'. This concern was evident in the other Churches also in the first and third worlds, although the manner of development and expression may have differed for Medellín (1968) and Geneva (1966), for Metz and Moltmann as well as for Gutiérrez and Alvez. These particular theological developments did not go unchallenged and there is a very lively debate within the Churches globally on the proper relationship between Theology and Social Analysis, between the Church's mission to the individual and the Church's mission to society. This debate can be reduced to simplistic caricatures. One form of caricature opposes those who insist exclusively on the responsibility of the Church for alleviating the historical socio-political needs of the deprived class in society and those who insist exclusively on the responsibility of the Church for the supernatural and eschatological needs of the individual souls of privileged and deprived. Caricatures do not allow for communication or debate. They have the value of highlighting certain strong tendencies which have validity in context and to scale but, isolated and exaggerated, result in mutual self-righteous rejection. The 'historical-social' and 'supernatural-eschatological' aspects of the Church's mission are most obviously intertwined for Catholics in the sacraments. In the return of theology to society and the ensuing controversy, insufficient attention has been paid to the sacraments. As a response to the seriousness with which John MacQuarrie has taken sacraments and sacramentality in his theological work and personal life, it may be appropriate to explore their significance in this context of theology and society.

In the renewal of sacramental theology, which in the 1950s and 1960s was associated in the Roman Catholic Church with Otto Semmelroth, Karl Rahner and Edward

Schillebeeckx, the sacraments were integrated with ecclesiology and finally with Christology. The Church as sacrament of Christ and Christ as sacrament of God were key-phrases in this renewal while the celebration of individual sacraments was understood as encounter with Christ in an ecclesial context. Vatican II, at least indirectly, endorsed and promoted much of this development. In a further insight Vatican II characterised the Church primarily by the presence of the mystery of God in *Lumen Gentium* (Contribution of the Church) and at the same time as the sacrament of the (comm)unity of humankind in *Gaudium et Spes* (Constitution on the Church in the World). The *mysterion* (*sacramentum*) of God's effective presence was also the sign, power and challenge for the emergence of all humanity as God's people. Sacrament is playing a critical symbolic and mediating role between God, Jesus Christ, Church and humanity in worldwide society.

The richness of this material for theology of sacraments and society is still largely unexplored. Meanwhile theology of society took a rather different turn with political and liberation theologies. As social theologies, the focus of these has been on word rather than sacrament, on the story of God's liberating activity in Israel and in Jesus as it illuminates and interacts with the stories of various deprived or oppressed peoples. The stories of Exodus and of Jesus' ministering to the poor and excluded, leading up to his death at the hands of the religiously and politically powerful, provide the paradigms for God's liberating activity in favour of today's poor and excluded. These paradigms are not just models of how God might act. They embody and express the actual liberating activity of God which grasps the authentic tellers of and the authentic listeners to the stories. The stories become saving stories, effective indications of God in action, parallel as they should be to the Catholic understanding of sacraments which in turn have their own narrative dimensions. Sacraments however do not figure strongly in this theology of society. For a variety of people they would be a supernatural placebo, keeping the down-trodden in their place. For others they are simply inauthentic in so far as they include oppressor and oppressed without any challenge to the oppressive structure. To include General Pinochet in the

78

Eucharist is repugnant to many Chileans who are oppressed or concerned for the oppressed. To exclude him would be repugnant to many others as a politicising of the very sacred mysteries. For significant anthropological students of religion, sacraments and ritual play an integrating stabilising role in society with inevitable support for the *status quo*. And this seems to apply to believers and unbelievers, conservatives and radicals among them. Any sharp contrast between the subversive potential of the Word of God with the conservative thrust of the sacraments, which might then issue in some Protestant-Catholic contrast, would be completely mistaken. The evangelical and fundamentalist Protestant groups, which emphasise so much the Word of God and largely underplay the sacraments, are frequently extremely conservative about political matters. Northern Ireland, South Africa and the southern states of the USA bear powerful testimony to that. Protestants and Catholics are divided on social and political issues in ways that are not accountable in terms of the Reformation divide or of the emphasis to be given to Word or Sacrament. It remains true, however, that in recent developments of social theology, so much of it Catholic, little attention has been paid to the theology of the sacraments.

The reference back of sacraments to Church and of Church to Christ as originating sacrament of God's presence to the world offers a useful starting-point for this exploration.

Ecclesial Events

Church as sacrament signifies and realises both Christ as the transforming presence of God to humanity and creation, and that transformed humanity and creation. It is both *sacramentum Christi* and *sacramentum mundi*. The individual sacraments, and especially the major sacraments of Baptism and Eucharist, are particular realisations of the sacrament that is Church. They are first of all ecclesial events, events in which the *ecclesia*, the called and gathered people, exercise their function of manifesting and realising the mystery of God. In Vatican II's constitution *Lumen Gentium* the first chapter on the Church as Mystery of God is followed by the chapter on the Church as People of God. It is in and through the people that the mystery is realised. It is in and

79

through and by the people that the particular mysteries of the individual sacraments are realised. In these sacramental events Church as Church, as *sacramentum Christi* and *sacramentum mundi*, fully and properly occurs. This would undoubtedly command wide acceptance among all Christians in regard to Eucharist and Baptism. Recent ecumenically agreed statements suggest that the convergence in regard to other 'minor' sacraments leads to an understanding of them also as ecclesial events along these lines. For the purposes of this discussion possible disagreements on 'minor' sacraments may be ignored. The argument will concentrate on Baptism and Eucharist within a generally ecumenical structure, although the theological framework will be of basically Catholic provenance.

In neo-scholastic Catholic theology of the sacraments, the event appeared confined to minister and recipient. The minister was ordained, the recipient or subject was not. Marriage was the exception in which the couple were regarded as ministers to one another although the mandatory presence of the priest as official witness could easily obscure the couple's role as ministers. Provision was also made for exceptional administration of baptism by the non-ordained in case of necessity. The overall impact was both individualist, particularly for the recipient, and clerical, in regard to the minister. The ecclesial community event whereby the Church realised and manifested itself as a mystery-bearing people was obscured and diminished. Vatican II's constitutions on liturgy and Church recovered the communal dimensions which recent theologians and liturgists had been emphasising and developing. The thrust of this communal dimension was to overcome both individualism and clericalism.

The return to community in sacramental theology and liturgical practice has enormous implications for the Church's self-understanding, worship, internal structures and activities. Some of these are already in evidence. Lay ministers of the Eucharist, including women, unthinkable twenty years ago, are commonplace today. This breach in clerical exclusivism with its further exposure of the community character of the Eucharistic celebration should not be dismissed as emergency exception or tokenism. In many places which have lay ministers there is no emergency; there are sufficient ordained ministers. Tokenism has curious resonances in the sacramental context. A token is itself a sign or symbol. In sacramental discourse talk of merely a symbol or a mere token carries elements of contradiction. Lay women and men bearing the Body of Christ with the ordained minister to the rest of the congregation is a new and powerful dimension of the sign or sacrament of the Eucharist in its realisation of the Church as community. It takes a step further the communal development of the vernacular liturgy with the priest re-joining the congregation in face-to-face relationship. It is more clearly in and through and for the gathered people that God's presence occurs. The liturgical leadership of the ordained minister is exercised in and with the people. The clericalism of a separate caste featuring a mystery man bordering on the magician becomes much less of a threat. The individualism of isolated recipients of the Eucharist yields in some degree to the sense of community event and celebration.

The fuller emergence of the community in the celebration of the Eucharist and the correlative reduction of clericalism illuminates the continually disturbing question of power in the Church. This is not an exclusively Roman Catholic question. And the disturbances takes on different forms in different ecclesial traditions, ranging from repression, a more Roman Catholic and Orthodox temptation, to fragmentation, a more Protestant temptation.

Power in the Church, as reflected in the celebration of the Eucharist and the other sacraments, relates to the Church's character as *sacramentum Christi* and *sacramentum mundi*. As sacrament of Christ, the Church is called to manifest and realise his way of exercising power. This way is in sharp contrast to that of worldly powers: 'not lording it over them as the Gentiles do', 'First last, and last first'. 'Servant of all'. Washing the disciples' feet is a primary symbol of Jesus' own leadership in service. The invocation of loving humble servant and service in contrast and challenge to the power-structures of the world may easily lose its edge as the old temptations to control and dispose reassert themselves. In almost counter-sacramental fashion Church leaders and structures have frequently reflected the worldly structures they were meant to challenge. Papacy, episcopacy, presbyterate council, synod and assembly can appear in style and substance very close to

81

imperial, feudal, or later models they were meant to challenge and subvert. Despite genuine and persistent attempts at reform, Church leaders and structures can too easily reverse the thrust of *sacramentum mundi* and *sacramentum Christi*. The way of the world, of power struggles and power structures, is reflected too closely in the Church. The way of Jesus Christ, of service structures and service struggles, is not adequately mediated to the world as challenge and transforming presence. Churches seem to have lost confidence in the efficacy of Jesus' way of leadership, above all for the world but also sadly for themselves. Sometimes they have to recover something of Jesus' service model from outside. The engagement of the Eucharistic community is necessary and communal decision-making may have to borrow from the practices of the secular world. Whether it can do so successfully without importing the party or lobby-system with its associated interest-groups and self-seeking is doubtful. Churches cannot escape the ambiguity of the human condition, communal and individual. The Synod of Bishops 1971 in dealing with the call to justice admonished the Churches on the weakness of their witness as long as their own structures were unjust, merely power-structures. The sacramental character of the Church, its summons and empowerment to offer the world an effective sign of transformed human community, constantly challenges it to confront its own power-seeking and develop beyond the current ambiguities into a more clearly serving community on the model of Jesus. Only so can it fulfil one of its basic services to human society, to be sacrament of the revolutionary relationships of power, authority and leadership which Jesus inaugurated.

Encountering Christ

The Church, in its sacramental nature and activity, and also the particular sacraments are compelled to examine more closely their relationship to Jesus Christ in his life, death and resurrection. A phrase, made popular through the writings of Edward Schillebeeckx in the 1950s and 1960s — 'encounter with Christ' — expresses this relationship effectively. Christ is the originating sacrament, the sign and realisation of God's presence from which the Church and the particular sacraments

82

derive their origin and continuing efficacy. Paul was the first great sacramental theologian and his discussion of Baptism in his letter to the Romans, Chapter 6, remains basic to the 'encountering Christ' theology of our own time.

'Encountering Christ' could prove the way to a wide range of contacts between sacraments and society. Once again it stresses the involvement with and of the whole Christ, the believing community through which Christ is encountered. Individualism cannot do justice to such an encounter. This applies obviously to the Eucharistic encounter. But the baptism of even one believer is also a community event. The community celebrates the arrival of a new member. The very ritual celebration acceptance in which in Paul's terms the neophyte is baptised into the death and resurrection of Jesus Christ is not an individualistic exchange of new member and minister, still less of new member and the individual Jesus Christ. The movement of acceptance and integration involves the believing community as a whole, which is drawn into a new participation in the death and resurrection of the Lord. This is commonly accepted in the theology of the Eucharist. The Eucharist itself, certainly in Roman Catholic theology and to some extent inspired by Thomas Aquinas, is regarded as the model and source of the other sacraments. Church, Eucharist and other sacraments realise their proper character as they share in the death and resurrection of the Lord. More accurately in this line of thinking the Church realises its proper character by sharing in the death and resurrection of the Lord through its celebration of (Word and) the sacraments. Encounter with Christ is always a community event and it is always by entry anew into the death and resurrection of the Lord.

In Baptism the resurrection of the baptised to the Lord is in and through the community. In the celebration of baptism the community enters into the death and resurrection, encounters Christ by surrendering to the baptised, the new member. There is a community openness, willingness to make place, to give service, to love, which involves movement of surrender, and which signifies and participates in Jesus' openness in love and service unto death.

Such an understanding of Baptism has clearly important inter-Church implications. Encountering Christ as it transcends the merely ecclesial cannot be thought of in denominational or divisive terms. Baptism into the death and resurrection of Christ is Baptism into the great Church which is the one Christ, the one body of Christ. Christian Churches have always accepted the validity of baptism performed in other traditions. A rather different point is being made here. Baptism is not just valid in the sense that a Church would accept a member baptised in another Church without requiring re-baptism. It is valid in the sense of embodying membership of the Christ which we all share in our different and divided Churches. More importantly still, the baptism of somebody into the Anglican Church, for example, involves the local Catholic, Presbyterian and Methodist communities in the celebration and acceptance of the new member into the one Body of Christ. Such celebration and acceptance implies openness and surrender to the new Christian and some external expression of that. The most obvious and practical would be representative participation in the Anglican Church on the occasion of the baptism. The further elaboration of this understanding and practice of every baptism as a shared Church event would have tremendous repercussions in the ecumenical movement. It would of course begin to make sense of the Church's call to be the sacrament of the unity of humankind as Vatican II emphasised, the *sacramentum mundi*. Its impact on the struggle for human unity would be one of manifestation and empowerment, in other words sacramental.

In the more confined world of Northern Ireland, with its overspill in Scotland, England and the Republic of Ireland, this understanding of Baptism presents a particular challenge. When asked what the Churches could do to help overcome the divisions in Northern Ireland, I sometimes, as a shock tactic, reply: 'They should stop baptising'. After the inevitable shock effect I go on to explain how the theological and ecclesiological significance of Baptism may be undermined by its social and political significance. Baptism of a new member into the local Church of Ireland or Presbyterian Church or Catholic Church has the same profound theological and ecclesiological significance. It is Baptism into the one Christ, the one great Church. All the Churches are called to recognise and celebrate this. The Catholic Church in Lisnaskea,

Co. Fermanagh, is called to be open to the Baptism of new members into the Church of Ireland and the Presbyterian Church in Lisnaskea. That openness involves a movement towards, a surrender to the new member in the community of the Church of Ireland. Such a movement should involve expression at the ritual itself. And the ritual expresses a challenge to whatever may, in history and politics, divide these communities which are united in faith and in Christ. It also carries empowerment with challenge in true sacramental fashion.

However, at this level of history and politics, of peoples' attitudes and division, the unity in Christ, the surrender to Christ, is obscured, if not rendered entirely futile. One of the traditional adages of sacramental theology and practice was that the sacraments should not be exposed to futility. Baptism in a particular Church, Protestant or Catholic, expresses integration into a particular historical community of Christians with its own cultural and political traditions which set it apart from and indeed against another community of Christians. Affiliation to the Unionist or Nationalist community is the other side of the Baptism event in Northern Ireland, which is in opposition to and sometimes in deadly conflict with integration into the Body of Christ. To preserve the sacraments from such futility should one not stop the practice of Baptism?

To carry on the practice while ignoring these implications and challenges would certainly promote a sense of futility. To cease the practice would be to lose the challenge and empowerment which the sacrament of Baptism offers to Christians at this crucial time in Northern Ireland. It is one of the few resources available to Christians as they seek to transcend their traditional and sometimes murderous divisions. It is precisely in the critical area of Northern Ireland that Christians must be prepared to take the ecumenical movement fully seriously and face the risks involved in taking Christ at his word and at his sacrament. The renewal of the ecumenical movement world-wide which such a move on Baptism in Northern Ireland would promote, should not be underestimated. More immediately and more for Northern Ireland and these islands it would begin to draw Christians together at their deepest level and detach them from automatic affiliation to hostile political factions. As Christians become more fully Christian, politicians could become more fully and properly political. The reverberating sacramental effect in that society would be tremendous.

Signs of the Kingdom

Sacraments as particular realisations of the Church, Church as sacrament of Christ and Crhist as sacrament of God provide a crude summary of the recent ways of sacramental theology. The presence and power of God which sacraments, Church and Jesus Christ ultimately mediate can in New Testament terms be spoken of as the Kingdom or Reign of God. The centrality of this Kingdom in Jesus' teaching and its return to the centre of so much theologising in this century facilitate a more profound reflexion on theology and society, on sacraments and society.

The fulfilment and transformation of humanity and cosmos through the creative and saving presence of God is what Jesus announces and inaugurates with the Kingdom. The already, the continuing but ambiguous, the yet-to-be are all dimensions of this creation-transformation which Jesus, Church and sacraments express and realise. The cosmic dimensions of the transformation are firmly indicated in the New Testament but without any clarity of form or definitiveness of time. The care of the universe to which current crises in the environment and ecology as well as the threat of nuclear destruction summon humanity, fit in with the sense of creation as gift to be celebrated and cherished which represents the best of the Hebrew and Christian traditions. The particular sacraments express their own sense of the value of such created cosmic gifts by integrating oil and water, bread and wine with human words and gestures in expressing and realising the presence of God, the Kingdom of God. As signs of God's presence, of his Kingdom, the sacraments show their respect for creation in itself and in its further dignity as mediating God's presence.

The creation and transformation of the cosmos reached its fullness in Jesus, in the human being who was Son of God. That fullness is to be shared by all humanity. The sacraments with the Church they particularise are to manifest, promote

86

and realise that fullness of all human beings as daughters and sons of God, sisters and brothers of Jesus Christ. The major sacraments of Baptism and Eucharist fulfil these roles in various ways. Two may be examined here, in the relationships of Christians to one another as expressive of all human relationships and in their relations to goods of the earth again as sacrament and sign for all.

Baptism as indicated earlier is the sacrament of entry into the community, as member of Christ, daughter or son of the Father. In that membership there are in principle no degrees and no divisions. Membership of Christ by entry into his death and resurrection may not be qualified or measured out in coffee spoons. There is a radical equality about Baptism into membership of Christ which no demands of organisation or responsibilities of leadership may reduce or obscure. To be first in the Kingdom is finally a self-contradictory request as Jesus hints. The Kingdom which surfaces in the Church has demolished such ranking. For the Church's own sake and for the sake of humanity to which it indicates the values of the Kingdom, the radical equality of Baptism must be kept to the forefront in theology and practice.

The world's divisions must go the same way as the world's rankings in face of Baptism. 'For as many of you as have been baptised into Christ have put on Christ. There is neither Jew nor Greek, there is neither bond nor free, there is neither male nor female: for you are all one in Christ Jesus (Gal. 3:27-8). In a world rent by such deep and deadly divisions, the call of the baptised to shed their hostile affiliations in the community of the baptised is an urgent demand of bearing witness to the Kingdom.

Relations with the cosmos and its resources enter intimately into relations between human beings and between Christians, even if the reduction of cosmic and human relations to economic is unacceptable. That the resources of the world are for all of humanity seems an obvious implication of the doctrines of creation and salvation. In the sign of the Eucharist, that is focused sharply in terms of food and drink, of bread and wine. The need of all Christians for Jesus' body and blood as bread and wine, maintains the pressure towards Eucharistic hospitality between the Churches. It moves into the world of economics and politics as a sign of the needs and rights of all, particularly of the starving, to access to the meat and grain mountains, the milk and wine lakes of this western world. The dialectic between Church and world, between sacrament and society, emerges very clearly in the call and the limitation to sharing heavenly and earthly food manifest in Church and world. The Kingdom appears also beyond all Church boundaries so that the Church is judged for both its Eucharistic and its economic parsimony. The world in turn has to learn from the creative generosity of God and of his son Jesus Christ which find expression in the symbol of the Eucharist.

Conclusion

The reflexions on sacraments and society developed here could and should be expanded for the major sacraments, in ways both creative and critical: creative in unveiling the richness of symbolism which Hebrew and Christian traditions have concentrated in our sacramental rituals; critical in enabling some thoughtful discrimination to be applied to the results of the creativity. Through the process of interaction with society, the sacraments as ecclesial events, encounters with Christ, and signs of the Kingdom may be discerned as presenting a challenge and empowerment to society, which society in its way offers to Church and sacraments.

PART II

Constructing
a Local Theology

9.

Irish Contexts
and Theological Methods

IN FURTHERING a theological analysis of the contemporary Irish situation, serious dialogue is required between theological methods developed in the historical and universal Church and the pressures and problems of the Irish context. The older, simpler way of applying universal methods (usually developed in Rome or Germany) to a particular situation like Ireland is nowadays seen as inadequate. Yet Ireland is not so utterly 'a place apart' that it does not share many of the pressures and problems of the wider world and cannot benefit from the theological developments occurring elsewhere. Not even in theology are there uniquely Irish solutions to Irish problems. Indeed a number of moves which have recently taken place in theology and theological method in first and third world countries offer, paradoxically, a general justification for developing a particularly Irish theology with its particular methods. It is with these moves that this investigation can most usefully begin. They are presented here by an Irish theologian who will inevitably reflect his Irish identity and preoccupations in his choice, order of priority and interpretation of these more broadly based moves. Irish theologising has already begun, if as yet only implicitly.

I. CONTEMPORARY MOVES IN METHOD

From the Universal to the Particular

Even twenty years ago, during Vatican II, it was taken for granted that a universal theology was possible, necessary and actually existed within the Catholic Church. Catholic theologians were not 'mega-stars' and did not enjoy schools of disciples after the fashion of Barth and Bultmann and their Protestant predecessors. Theology was a service to the Catholic community, mainly engaged in expounding rather than exploring its doctrinal heritage and subordinate to the official teachers of the universal Church. Theology could and should be like the Latin mass: the same everywhere. This was never of course simply true. The diversity of the Patristic and Medieval periods may have been greatly reduced but was not eliminated by the demands of the Counter-Reformation. Even in the threatening nineteenth century, various German theologians at Tübingen and elsewhere, with Newman in England, provided counter-poles to the centralising tendencies of Rome and its theological mode. Yet the theologies of Tübingen, of Newman and of early twentieth-century successors had at least a universalising tendency. They could be the theology of every local Church and every believer. The further developments in the mid-twentieth century in French and German language theologies, especially with the hesitant emergence of fresh giants like Congar, de Lubac, Chénu and Rahner, led to the upheavals of Vatican II but with theologising still in that predominantly universalising mode and theology in its all-conquering European form.

Yet the seeds of differentiation were already sown. European theologians and theologies were becoming more obviously diverse and divergent. The differences between Congar and Rahner and Küng were becoming obvious, exaggerated and distorted no doubt by the star system of a theology becoming show-business. There were more important sources of difference evident in the diversity of the Council fathers themselves, between first and third world bishops for example and within these groupings also. The African bishops and Churches could not be taken together with the Latin American despite their third world status, while the Western Europeans and North Americans were far apart on many issues before and indeed after the Council. The paradoxical achievement of the Council, for theology, was to encourage local Churches and their theologians while promoting a new and exciting sense of the Catholicity of the Church. The Council vision, theological assertiveness and local need achieved their most significant breakthrough at the Latin American Bishops' Conference at Medellín in 1968. With its acceptance of 'liberation theology' as appropriate to the Latin American Churches' needs, the move from universal to particular theology received official endorsement and a new range of energy and research. Meanwhile the 'liberal' European theology which had prevailed at Vatican II was being seriously challenged by the 'political theology' of John Baptist Metz and Jurgen Moltmann. The roots of this lay in social-political analysis, and this gave it a particularity, historical and social, akin to if not as radical as that of Latin American 'liberation theology'.

The particularising spread, regionally, socially, racially and sexually. From Dar-es-Salaam to Sri Lanka to the Philippines to Japan the need to develop faith reflexion within the concrete milieu of the particular local believing community was freely recognised. And the local setting was not proving particular enough. Social location, more sharply revealed in social analysis and in the growing awareness of the social structure of cognition, became a distinctive theological — or, more accurately, a distinctive theologians' — locus. The particularity of theology was influenced by the socio-economic setting of its practice and practitioners. 'Black theology' and 'feminist theology', both emanating from the United States of America, were important examples of the particularity of theology derived from historical, cultural and socio-economic analysis of the place of black Americans and American women in their white, male-dominated society.

The particularity which characterises these theologies is perhaps the greatest single change in theological practice in the last twenty years. Yet it should be seen in a historical context, in which, for all the white male European dominance of Christian theology over two thousand years, creative changes occurred and destructive tendencies emerged under the pressure of particular circumstances of time and place and people. The defeat of the Judaising party in New Testament times is the first critical break with the dominance of one interpretation of Christian belief and practice, of one theology. (According to Karl Rahner the second really critical change has occurred in our own time: like the global village, the Church can become truly catholic.) Over the centuries politics, cultures and personalities gave us a series of theologies particular to an age and region, although they were usually taken to be universal in thrust if not accepted as such. It is only with the rise of historical consciousness in our own time that the particularity and relativity of previous theologies could be properly recognised and assessed. Such historical awareness did not quite prepare the Church of Vatican II for the depth and range of the particular theologies now available. Their very variety and the undoubted strength of some of them provide powerful resources for growth of faith in all of us. They have their own ambiguities also, not unrelated to the ambiguities of earlier theological achievements. Their very success for a particular region or group makes them unreceptive to the criticism they will certainly need for further healthy development. They could become exclusivist and excluding, reducing the exploration of the faith of all who accept Jesus to the faith and exploration of one group defined in socio-political, racial and sexual terms. The other side of this temptation is to treat one particular theological achievement as mandatory for all, yielding paradoxically to a new form of universalism and imperialism. These are not temptations which such young theologies should become preoccupied with. They are merely the inevitable temptations which they have seen succeed in the white, male, Western theology — that theology which they are rejecting for themselves.

The theological move from the universal to the particular takes different forms, historical and geographical, socio-economic, racial and sexual, as I have indicated and will return to later. The move remains a move within the historical tradition of Christianity and the Catholic ambit of the Church as the believing community world-wide. Particularity does not involve total separation between theologies or traditions or communities. Continuity, unity in differentiation, is both a grace and a challenge which believers, theologians and church-leaders have to consciously and persistently accept. The mutual excommunication to which Christians are sometimes tempted is a failure to take fully seriously both the comm-unity of faith and the differentiation of theologies. Some first world reactions to some Latin American theologies, like certain male reactions to 'feminist' theologies seem unable to accept this grace and challenge. This failure can be found on both sides, in fact.

Against the background of this generally enriching move in contemporary theology, from the universal to the particular, Irish theologians are challenged, encouraged and assisted in attempting a faith analysis of their own situation. More specific aspects of the move will be discussed in the following sections while some relevant Irish particulars will be confronted in the final part of this chapter.

From the Privileged to the Deprived

For all its claims to universality, traditional theology has always been particular, particular to a dominant culture (Hebrew, later Greek and then Latin), to a dominant political grouping (the role of Emperors and Kings in Western or Eastern, Roman or Anglican theology), to a dominant profession (the clergy), to a dominant sex (male), to a dominant race and class (white middle class), to a dominant set of institutions (seminaries in recent Catholic history, universities in recent Protestant history). The dominated did not figure in these theological developments. They might be the objects of the theological analysis or education (in Paulo Freire's terms) but never the subjects. Theology, like history, has been written by the victors. Its particularity in this respect was denied by the victors in their claims to universality and objectivity. It was not recognised by the victims either, in their final victimisation as they internalised the views of the victors.

This is a brief and necessarily crude account of how theology became the possession and the instrument of the privileged while the deprived were excluded. Theology was not alone in this. Other cultural and intellectual enterprises endured the same fate. Yet the possession was never complete and always threatened, in culture generally because of the restlessness of the human spirit of enquiry and creativeness, and in theology more specifically because of its inherently subversive subject matter: the victim Jesus Christ as the presenter of the unpossessable and uncontrollable God. Despite historical appearance, the movement of theology has not been downhill all the way since Calvary. The continuing renewals in Church life have been at once the product and the source of theological renewal, which has continued to reach out to the dispossessed despite its powerful possessors. The theological significance of the monastic movements in the Patristic era, of the mendicants in medieval times, of the socially excluded and marginalised Wycliffites and Hussites and anabaptists prior to and during the Reformation period, of the resurgence of the ways of poverty in the renewal of religious orders at the Counter-Reformation and after, kept theology, at least in part, in touch with the deprived. But it was only in part, and in small part, as is shown by the interpretation, by European Christian minds, and the fate, at European Christian hands, of American Indians, of African slaves and of the women of the world. These omitted and forgotten people become a focus for the 'subversive Christian memory' of J. B. Metz and for the call to Christian solidarity with the victims, developed by Matthew Lamb and others. The move from the privileged to the deprived in theology reflects the Church's option for the poor, heralded at Medellín in 1968.

Beginning with the deprived and the victims, to share their sufferings and oppression, their perspective, understanding and aspiration, is to have a very different view of the world, its development and destiny, its origins, destructiveness and fulfilment, its Creator, Saving and Fulfilling God. The view from Calvary, from the place of the skull of the victim, is inevitably different from that of the *cathedra* or chair of professor, emperor or even bishop. That differing view of the victim will include a different Christian hope, the hope in which and by which we are saved. A different hope involves a different view of salvation, of the mission and work of Jesus Christ, of the Kingdom of God which he proclaimed and inaugurated. The different view emanating from the Latin American poor, North American blacks and initially North American women, has expressed the major theological move from the universal to the particular in terms of the move from the privileged to the deprived. Further characteristics of this significant move, especially the relationship between theory and praxis, contemplation and action will be dealt with in a later section. Meanwhile it is convenient to take up a move somewhat different in origin and character but related to the privileged-deprived move in the exercise of theology: that is the move from systematic to narrative.

A common reaction to change in theology as in other disciplines or departments or life is to say, 'In so far as it has anything useful to offer it is not new; in so far as it is new it has nothing useful to offer.' There has been a strong temptation to this kind of reaction among systematic, and as they would see it, more hard-nosed theologians, in face of the recent emphasis on narrative as mode as well as source of theology.

That well-worn object of caricature, based on numerous models in reality, the manual of systematic (Catholic) theology, was characterised by an ahistorical abstract form of thinking which presented Christian faith as an elaboration of abstract and conceptual doctrines. In the beginning was the word of Denzinger! And a very limiting and controlling word it was: limiting in its appeal to the logically intellectual and abstractly verbal, controlling in its invocation and imposition of the supreme teaching authority in the Church, Pope or Council. The elaboration involved some attention to the historical development of doctrine, but always in religious and philosophical terms, scarcely ever in terms of the personalities, their strengths and weaknesses, and their stories, and never in terms of influential political, economic, social and broader cultural forces (broader, that is, than philosophical linguistic considerations). The exciting theological developments of the fourth and fifth centuries were not, in their presentation, given the narrative form that could embrace all the forceful personalities and all the influential forces, both successful and defeated. The history of doctrine, of dogmatic or systematic theology, tended to be a history of ideas, orthodox and unorthodox. Any further explication, for a contemporary audience, of Nicea, Chalcedon, Trent or Vatican I, remained within this genre, a deduction of further ideas and assertions from the officially recognised ideas and assertions of Councils and Popes. Development of doctrine was curiously sealed off from the religious experience and needs of the wider believing people. Theology was the (intellectual) sport of clerics. The early Dietrich Bonhoeffer, subsequently to adopt a radically different stance, wrote in a powerful image as applicable to systematic

97

theology as to its churchly master, 'Like a sealed train travelling through foreign territory, the Church goes on its way through the world.' (The sealed trains of Lenin to join and take over the Revolution, or of Jewish victims on their way to the death camps, were hardly in his mind just then.) For Catholics the sealed train was, however, opened decisively at Vatican II. But this had been prepared for by the breaking open of its theology, particularly from the systematic to the more historical and narrative mode in patristic *ressourcement* and biblical studies. The Catholic recovery of the Bible as central (replacing Denzinger) was decisive for the later developments at Vatican II and prepared the way for the particular manner of theology called narrative.

The renewal of biblical studies in the Catholic tradition, after the freeze which followed the modernist crisis, found the Protestant developments particularly in Europe and above all in Germany accelerating beyond the literary analysis which had attended to the complete text and, if appropriate, to its narrative sweep. Historical, form and later redaction criticism had to be rapidly assimilated by Catholic scholars in ways that restored the bible and biblical studies to the centre of Catholic scholarship but without the sensitivity to story or narrative which might have been expected. 'The Eclipse of Biblical Narrative' was partly reinforced by developing existentialist and then structuralist handling of the text and by the socio-economic study of its background. The valuable achievements of all these approaches and their continuing and more sophisticated employment has not prevented the return of the text as text — and complete text — and the re-emergence of attention to the narrative character and force of biblical texts and of theological writing generally.

The details, complex and far-reaching, of the continuing story of biblical and theological textual analysis cannot be pursued here. The acceptance of the force of the narrative in the search for Christian understanding and engagement reaches through Old and New Testament writings, through particular storied events like the Exodus and Jesus and the Good Samaritan, to mould a particular way of doing theology entitled narrative theology.

The concern of this essay in theological method is with how narrative operates as a mode of doing theology in contrast to the systematic and conceptual way. It clearly shares in the move from the universal to the particular. Stories are about particular people and events. They are told by and to particular people with their own (hi)stories which already fashioned the story-tellers and story-hearers in ways that make them more or less ready to adopt and adapt the stories as they are told. In a perspective that can be valid and illuminating, the meeting of people, individuals or groups, is an intertwining of the stories, past and present, by which they have been shaped and which they have shaped. People are, at any point, their own stories but they are also able to tell and to listen to other stories. The group is a fascinating and unfinished fabric of people's stories and the group must be finally enlarged to include the whole human community, past, present and future.

For Christians the critical story is the story of Jesus and the first disciples as recorded in the New Testament. But Christians have always recognised with Jesus, the first disciples and the first recorders, that his story and theirs is part of an older continuing story, the story of Israel. The final break between Christian and Jew, some time after the fall of Jerusalem, may be understood in one sense as their inability to continue combining their stories. Jesus, or at least the disciples, had so radically changed the story of Israel for later Jews that they could no longer recognise it as their own, the story they had told from Moses to Jesus and continued to tell subsequently. The Christian and Jewish peoples, with their diverging stories and incompatible story-shaped worlds, went their separate ways with drastic consequences for both in later times.

Each of us a story, each shaped by stories, each with stories to tell: to accept this as one useful and true description indicates why and how we chose foundation — or at least critical — stories for our lives at different levels, at the level of ultimate relations which we call religious, at the level of ethnicity and nationality, at the level of locality and family. So the stories may include those of Moses or Jesus or Mahomet, those of the British Empire or of Indian or African colonisation, of Ireland 1690 or Ireland 1916, of the fatal fame of the Kennedys or the 'No Name in the Street' of James Baldwin. The stories of the victors and the victims, like James Baldwin's black brothers, sisters and ancestors or Catholics in contemporary Lithuanian history-books, are written out of the story. The TV soap-operas practice exactly the same technique with an unsuccessful character or player.

Because we are people with our own stories we learn and develop, change, even convert, through listening to or reading and at the same time entering into the stories of others. Historical criticism in its various sophisticated and objectifying forms provides the necessary partner to the literary criticism whereby we are enabled to establish in varying degrees both the truth and the meaning of a particular story. The truth and the meaning of *The Brothers Karamazov* relate closely in form to the truth and the meaning of the *Book of Job* or the story of the Good Samaritan. The Gospels and particular narrative sections of the Hebrew Scriptures have a more complex relation of truth and meaning and a more profound potential for drawing us into the story, revealing reality to us, converting us. Truth, meaning, revelation and conversion, as derived by us from the story of Exodus and supremely from the story of Jesus, require the skills and techniques of historical scholarship but with attention to the narrative character of the text and of ourselves as well as the awareness in ourselves of broad categories of human love and trust, suffering and salvation, as raising ultimate or religious questions. Without awareness of these dimensions of our own stories we will be unable to combine historical and literary criticism, unable to accept and share the truth and meaning of other persons and events by entering their story in the text.

The narrative mode of theology ensures that we recognise the participatory demands made on the student of the Scripture texts and the clash as well as the emergence of stories and interests which that study may and frequently will provoke. By clash and convergence the sceptical or suspicious and the trusting approach to hermeneutics co-operate in arriving at the fuller truth. The shared vision needs the critical, sceptical visionary to keep the vision honest. The attempts to evaluate and relate clashing narratives and visions — of Unionist Protestant and Nationalist Catholic in Ireland — by first relating each to the Gospel narrative in convergence and divergence will test the usefulness of the narrative method as an Irish method of theology.

In all this discussion, while the emphasis on the narrative is important, the differences and detachment from the conceptual and systematic can be greatly exaggerated. The narrative way to truth needs the conceptual tools of historical and literary criticism as I have indicated. All discussion of narrative as narrative, or of a particular story which does not stop at telling the story, is conceptual, analytic, systematic. Within the story itself the language and concepts of more obviously systematic discourse are very evident. One has only to try telling any story in utterly particular concrete terms to realise that universal, abstract and evaluative language cannot be avoided. To be *neighbour* to somebody, as the *Good* Samaritan was, and so fulfil the *primary law* of *love*, is to employ the language common to various kinds of discourse. Dialogue in these terms between Jesus and his questioners introduced and concluded the story of the man who fell among robbers, set in the wider story of Jesus and his questioners. The Gospel accounts of Jesus' life and teaching are full of such stories, and images. Paul of course ignores for the most part any narrative framework while he remains a critical source of Christian truth and meaning. The recovery of narrative is an important enrichment of theological method, in the general framework of the move from the universal to the particular. It must not be exaggerated and isolated as a self-contained and self-sufficient method of theology.

From Narrative and Vision to Performance and Experiment

Telling the story (announcing the good news) and so entering the vision, shaping the vision, through convergence of stories and conversion of people, is the classic pattern of presenting and accepting the Gospel. Reflexion on that vision, theology or contemplation, remaining close to the narrative in its linguistic character and systematic potential has proved the predominant mode of theologising from Paul to Augustine to Aquinas to Barth to Rahner. The Word contemplated becomes the Word explored, analysed, justified, 'explained' and taught. Theologians at their best were contemplatives and not activists. Or so the conventional story goes. It was a little more complicated, as the hyperactive Paul with his dense and elaborate theologising might have indicated. But then he was and remained a Hebrew despite the Roman citizenship and Greek modes of thought and expression. Augustine was no isolated, inactive worker either. Many of the late influential theologians like Barth and Bonhoeffer were influenced in their theology by intense pastoral or even political activity. The overall description of theology as contemplative, closer to prayer than to pastoral or social/political engagement is probably true. The recent shift to activity or performance as a 'constituent element' of theologising, of analysing and understanding the faith, is characteristic of our own times and specifically of that form of theology known as 'Liberation Theology' and originating in Latin America. Doing the truth, learning through doing, faith as commitment, faith as discipleship and so essentially performative: these are more traditional expressions which have been rediscovered and critically developed if not transformed. The performance or doing is seen as service of the Kingdom, faith active, but in a critique of historical society, a commitment to its transformation and engagement with that transformation. Social analysis directed to social change enters into the reality of faith and the reflexion on it called theology. Praxis, critical engagement with the transformation of society, a word not always so clear in its meaning or so consistent in its use, is given priority over theory, *theoria* as vision/contemplation and reflexion on vision, *theoria* as theology.

The historical, analytic, socially transforming and liberating thrust of faith and its understanding in theology, as proposed by liberation and political theologians, goes beyond the personal performative character which the faith of Christian disciples was always regarded as having. That performative character could and should have been recognised as communal in the ecclesial sense and as social in its commitment to the coming of the Kingdom in society. Such theological potential has been realised in a particular way by contemporary theologians through their conscious engagement with the deprived in society as a first expression of Christian faith, and their employment of modern methods of social analysis in exposing the structures of privation and the requirements to overcome them. Whether the social analysis is to be described as Marxist or more generally socialist

102

is partly a question of terminology, partly a question of which particular liberation and political theologian one is discussing and partly depends on how far one recognises that certain kinds of analaysis associated with Marx have entered into the generally accepted intellectual practices of the contemporary world. However, the description by theologians themselves or by their critics of this theology as Marxist can be misleading intellectually and unnecessarily divisive.

The other temptation and accusation faced by such theologians is that of substituting political salvation in history for eternal salvation; the human in origin, history and resources for the divine; the historical and horizontal for the eschatological and transcendent. They are not the first theologians to be exposed to this temptation and this accusation. It would be surprising if they survived the temptation better than others, including some of their critics, whose practical horizons are often time-bound and political, although the temporal and political terms are ecclesial rather than social. The identification of the Church with the Kingdom or more seriously and commonly its substitution for the Kingdom; the good of the Church obscuring or replacing the good and the truth of the service and liberation offered by Jesus and so yielding to the truth of domination; these are characteristic temptations of church-leaders and theologians which are not always and never fully resisted.

Critical evaluation of the move to the practical and performative by theology deserves careful but fair evaluation. It must be set in the perspective of the active following of discipleship and related to the limitations of more conventional theology and to the fact that all theology has a political significance; it affects people's attitudes to the political situations in which they live, encouraging and sometimes enabling them to ignore them, accept them, criticise them, even change them. This is true of Augustine, Aquinas, Luther, Calvin, Barth and Rahner as it is of Bonino, Gutiérrez or Metz.

There is one final point about the moves to the performative which is given less attention than it deserves. These could as easily develop an infallibility of orthopraxis as of orthodoxy without the same criteria and safeguards. At one extreme this could lead to intolerance and dictatorship, a temptation which has afflicted many left and right-wing regimes in this century. At the other extreme it could lead to paralysis. Unless one were absolutely sure that this was the right thing to do, morally and pragmatically, one would do nothing. It is here that God-given powers of human imagination and creativity need to be invoked in experimenting with ways forward. Such experiments involving people's lives may not be undertaken lightly or in an unprepared way. Yet every human life, every life of faith, every community and every person has to learn ways forward to the uncomprehensible God who comes to meet us by trying out what seems most appropriate at the time. This is true of personal, spiritual, liturgical, ecclesial and interchurch life, as it is of political life for Christians in their commitment to the promotion of the Kingdom. The fear of failure which can paralyse the best of people eventually derives from a lack of faith and trust and love. The Spirit which moved over the waters and was breathed into the dust of the earth, which led Jesus into the desert and finally up the hill of Calvary, knows something of the historical failure of even divine 'experiments' and how they may be eventually turned into the triumph of resurrection. It is that creative and experimental Spirit which Christians and theologians are called to follow. By seeking to understand the Spirit's past activity they recognise the creative experimental character of that activity and its summons to, as well as illumination of, present and future experimental response to the demands of the Kingdom in Church and society. In a way parallel to, but obviously not identical with, the physical sciences Christians and all human beings are called to build on previous successful (and failed) experience/experiment, to develop by trying out and attempting to move beyond the present in its achievements and limitations. Care is demanded in making these attempts at the new but so is courage. And success is not guaranteed. The ministry of Jesus from Nazareth to Calvary, of great Christian and non-Christian successors from Peter and Paul to Dietrich Bonhoeffer, Mahatma Gandhi, Martin Luther King and Oscar Romero is evidence enough for that. But without these crucial experiments of apparently failed historical heroes, humanity and Christianity would cease to grow towards the inbreaking God of Jesus Christ. The performance and experiments of genuine saints and heroes provoke and reflect the vision, as they inspire and shape the inspiring and shaping narrative.

Beyond the Particular

The move from the universal to the particular which takes the various forms described above does not abolish the value of the universal or general, although it does qualify that value very considerably. It is still possible and necessary to communicate theologically across the boundaries of culture, history, social and political setting, race, sex and class. (The move to feminist theology from exclusively male or patriarchal I consider a special example of the move from the privileged to the deprived.) One particular theology may, at least in the light of Jesus Christ and his mission, never be so exclusive as to prevent communication with another. Communication involving some community of faith and expression are basic to the achievement of Jesus Christ. There are common terms and shared understandings which Christians have to work at and only partially achieve but which they cannot ignore.

The moves in recent theology have not all been one way. There have been moves from the more particular to the more general. To some extent this is an aspect of the move from narrative to performance where performance is understood in more than personal terms to be that of the Christian community or *ecclesia* rather than that of individual disciples. The *Church* must perform as Church, not just the individual Christians. And the Church must perform for *humanity* or at least the particular defined society and not just its own members. Theology is an ecclesial or community exercise, not a personal one as so many recent theologians of an existentialist or personalist tendency might appear to suggest. It is for the world, the larger society, not just for the Church itself.

A further enlargement of the theologising community emerges in the growth of inter-Church relations and the recognition by these Churches of their common mission to proclaim and serve the Kingdom. The new subject of theological activity is the Churches, not the Church. Theology must be not simply ecclesial, but ecumenical. Given the divisions of the Church and in particular the diversity of their authority structures, many people find it difficult to conceive of an effective ecumenical theology. To abandon one's Catholic or Anglican or Orthodox or Presbyterian tradition, as the critics see it, in the name of some hybrid or some lowest common denominator, sacrifices religious and intellectual integrity. And it would be precisely a failure in integrity to abandon these traditions, but we all belong to an older and wider tradition which ante-dates the major divisions and has survived beyond them. Recognising this, Catholics in particular, who take seriously the Decree of Ecumenism as the starting-point of a whole process of inter-Church relations in which other Christians are accepted as incorporated in Christ and other Churches are accepted as Churches, have to embrace the tradition of the wider and older *ecclesia* in service to the future and fuller *ecclesia*. Ecclesial theology becomes ecumenical in that perspective.

The further demands on theology and theologians take them beyond theological traditions and reflexion on them into all the challenge of other disciplines, including the new disciplines generated by the human and the physical sciences and their technological capacity. The Christian understanding of the human and divine has to meet the extraordinary technical achievements of the artificial reproduction of human beings and the artificial intelligences of machines. Any confining of theological activity to the particularly religious tradition of humankind, even in a way that reaches from Judaism and Christianity across the spectrum of world religions, evades what for theologians must be some of the most important challenges and potentially enriching achievements of the contemporary world. The theologian, even in his 'religious' particularity, lives on the boundary of disciplines and achievements which continually summon him beyond this particularity.

II. CENTRAL, CRITICAL AND TRANSFORMING TRUTHS

In the second part of this chapter I wish to examine a few aspects of the Jewish-Christian tradition that are central to the tradition itself, and which in their critical and transforming power have a role to play in recent methodological moves.

I had thought of using the terms myth-model-metaphor in the title but feared that the attempt to do justice to the richness and variety of their current usage would prove too large a task just here. For all the explanations, their fundamental work of communicating fundamental truth(s) might be ignored or misunderstood. However I will be conscious of their usage and value and invoke them at times in ways that will be properly illuminating.

Two of the truths or themes which I have chosen have a high profile in contemporary theology, although not necessarily in the same theological movement. 'Israel and Exodus' for example has proved specially fruitful in the development of Latin American liberation theology and its associates. 'Jesus and the Kingdom' is pervasive of much modern theology although it has received more attention in relation to its scriptural roots than in relation to its present implications. The third, 'Creation and New Creation', has not yet received the theological emphasis it might, although clearly the sensitivity to ecological issues now at work in theology has a bearing on it.

The truths themselves are expressed in conjunctive form which is meant to indicate a living relationship, a dynamic interchange. This is not quite what Karl Barth calls 'Catholicism's accursed "and",' because it is not a holding together of two apparently incompatible aspects of the one Truth but an attempt to underline two different poles in interaction, a form of dialectic — to invoke another piece of the old jargon — although neither term properly fits thesis or antithesis, and synthesis is not properly achievable. The notion of continuing dynamic relationship is what is important although the two polar realities in all three cases fit awkwardly into the notion of comparable, contrasting and relating entities.

Israel and Exodus

When it comes in the Hebrew scriptures as we have them, the story of Exodus is a story, and a story of particularisation. From the Creator God and the human fathers of humanity in Genesis we move through Abraham the father of a great nation and countless descendants to the call of Moses and particular choice of a particular people by a particular God,

107

'You shall be my people and I shall be your God.' The vindication of that Godhead lay in the liberation from the oppression of Egypt. The covenanted response required of the chosen people was awakened in the Decalogue and the laws. Israel, set free and established as God's people, was the mighty act of God comparable to, indeed for Israelites greater than, his earlier dealings with Abraham and Noah and his original act of creation.

The subsequent history of Israel in its failures to live out the covenanted relationship between God and his people provides new opportunities for the faithful creativity of God as he loves, invites, corrects, punishes, protects and vindicates his people in action for the present and in promise for the future. Exodus is the apex. It constitutes the central divine achievement in Israel's past and its guarantee for the future. The mighty will continue to be put down while the slaves and the oppressed will be liberated and saved.

The specific historical character and detail of the Exodus story may never be satisfactorily established. Such historical work must continue and will enrich our understanding of Israel's history and its historical faith. In the context of the Pentateuch the historical or actual event-based character of the Exodus was no doubt important to successive generations of Israelites but their historical categories and methods were not ours. By their own categories and methods, which were not simply lacking in differentiation between different modes of stories and legends as a comparison between early Genesis and the Book of Exodus shows, the Book of Exodus was their foundation character, mythical in the sense of containing the basic truths of their identity, of their relationship with God and of their establishment as God's people through Liberation.

The telling of the Exodus story as central to understanding what God is doing in the world, the surrender to the story's transforming call and power to enter into the liberation of the oppressed, constitutes a central and powerful theme in current liberation theology. The mighty act of God in which Christians, who claim to believe in this God of Israel, must share is still the liberation of the oppressed. The bondage of Egypt still goes on around the world and the address of God to Moses must be heard and acted on by Christians. That is the call and response of faith. The work for liberation in response to that call is faith, and reflexion on the work is theology. But the work, the engagement comes first; orthopraxis precedes orthodoxy.

The value and attractiveness of this analysis is clear. Oppression continues. It is always in defiance of the will and the way of the God of Moses and of Jesus Christ. Their followers must challenge that oppression and seek to overcome it. In this task they will be responding to God at work in our world, sharing his illuminating and empowering grace. Liberation and exodus from oppression and slavery have emerged in a striking way for contemporary Christians as a critical discipleship task. Listening to and entering the story of the Israelites' Exodus from Egypt inspires and enlightens liberating Christians. Narrative and praxis of the particular Hebrew people connect with the narrative and praxis of a hundred modern parallel peoples in critical and transforming truth.

The value of the Exodus story today requires continuing theological appreciation but also theological critique. The desert experience of the Hebrews, the conquest of the land of Canaan and the subsequent development of Israel have many shadow, oppressive sides. The victim becomes victor and too easily turns victimiser in the history of Israel as in so much other human history. The ambiguities of all human political situations and achievements may not be invoked to paralyse the moves towards Liberation. They may not be ignored, either, without paying the price of identifying the new victors as simply divinely blessed, no longer in need of criticism. This is how new victims will inevitably emerge as well as the inevitably new establishment-God, sharing many of the idol-qualities of the former establishment-God.

The appeal to Exodus did not start with Latin American liberation theologians or the oppressed there. The self-identification of North of Ireland Unionists and South African Afrikaaners has always included Exodus as part of their myth and identity, at obvious cost to North of Ireland Nationalists and South African blacks. The victims (as Afrikaaners saw themselves) became victors and then turned victimisers with a vengance, as the new 'victims' see it. It is this ambiguity of history, ineradicable from the eschatological perspective of Christians, which demands constant critical evaluation of the application of the Exodus story in current political situations. More systematically the Christian call to identify with the oppressed and to seek to overcome the oppression in all its depth and urgency requires an effective, thought-through and comprehensive response which will not allow the easy substitution of one set of victims for another or ignore in particular cases mutual victimisation; God is with all the victims and the only complete divine victory embraces the whole family of human beings. Of course the worst victims have priority with God, and the victims closest to us, whom we might somehow serve, have a certain priority for us. But God's priorities are not always easily discernible and the manner of responding requires as much head as heart. Exodus is a continuing process of liberation in history which summons us all to the destruction of political, economic, racial and sexist bondage. It is an urgent yet delicate task. Retelling the story of Exodus of Israel from Egypt is, as the scientists say, a necessary but not a sufficient condition for fulfilling our liberating task.

Jesus and the Kingdom

In its Old Testament context the story of Exodus signals a move from universal to the particular. In current usage it also signals the move from systematic to narrative, from narrative to performance, from sacred to secular and from Church interests to social and political interests. The renewed attention to Jesus as distinct from Christ also emphasises particularity. Jesus the Jew and Jesus the man from Nazareth draws attention to his ethnic, religious and local particularity. The systematic attractiveness found in John and Paul has yielded to or at least been balanced by the story of Jesus as story. Jesus as story is becoming, if it has not become, something of a theological cliché. It does emphasise the personal and historical particularity of Jesus and present his life and activity as normative for active and reflexive disciples, for a disciples' theology.

Jesus was not bound by his particularity. The caring father from whom he claimed his origins and his mission and with whom he saw his destiny was the Father of Abraham and Moses, of Samaritans as well as Jews, of those beyond the tradition of Israel since he was the creator of the lilies of the field and of the whole natural world. This Father's particular mission for Jesus 'Last of all he sent his own son' (Mt. 21 : 37 par.), was formulated by Jesus in terms of proclaiming and inaugurating the final Kingdom (Mt. 4 : 17 par.). The particularity of Jesus and his mission had universal and ultimate significance for all people, past, present and to come — people who had longed for this day, (Jn. 8 : 56), the people Jesus addressed and who accepted or rejected him (Mt. 22 : 24f.) and the people who later would have liked to have seen his day, but still believe even though they do not see him (Jn. 20 : 29).

The universal sweep of Jesus' Kingdom illuminates again the paradox of divine-human relationships, of the very human itself. The human being in his unicity and uniqueness, in the depth of his particularity can count himself king of infinite space. The restless self-transcendence which continually opens him up beyond himself can never rest until it rests in the ultimately Transcendent God who reaches to human beings in the Kingdom embodied by Jesus in history but extends beyond any particular history to encompass all. The eschatological, transhistorical thrust of the Kingdom is the guarantee to all history that it has meaning. It is the divine commitment to the forgotten of history, to the excluded, the deprived, the victims and all those without a name or a role in history that their unicity and uniqueness have not been arbitrarily lost. They are not failed experiments of a blind nature or a capricious creator.

The dynamic interaction between the particular Jesus and the universal Kingdom continues in history between the community of Jesus' disciples, the Church in its divine particularities and the universal, ultimate Kingdom. The Church is not the Kingdom but its sign, preacher, promoter as well as its historical realisation in history. That Church subordinate to the Kingdom is frequently tempted to identify itself with Kingdom now and in this place, e.g. Ireland. The temptation is not always resisted, so that a community called to humble service takes on the form of dominant power. The direction of Philippians 2 is reversed. The self-emptying of Jesus yields to the self-inflation of the Church. In the contemporary world one of the major graces available in face of that temptation is Church-division and the presence of different

Churches. With that kind of history of division and the continuing failures to overcome it, the Churches have every
reason to be modest in assessing their relation to the Kingdom.
This is particularly true in Ireland where divided Church-
affiliation is not the cause of — but does compound — political divisions which issue in mutual destructiveness. Whatever
the good intentions of Church-people, very little has been
achieved by the Churches in disentangling political affiliation
and Church affiliation or in reversing the reinforcing role
which the Churches appear to play in so many Irish divisions.

The humiliation of the Churches in face of Irish divisions,
if it could be recognised as such, would be the grace needed
to convert us to a deeper apprecation of our role of modest
service to a Kingdom which transcends all Church boundaries.
The humbling grace of Church-division is available world-
wide in helping to overcome a triumphalism which at best
concentrates on the presence of Christ risen while ignoring
Jesus crucified, and at worst identifies itself with the fullness in history of the presence of the risen Christ, the full
historical expression of the Kingdom.

For Irish and contemporary theologians in general, fuller
attention to Jesus in his servant and suffering roles will
facilitate their work of critical reflexion on the praxis of
discipleship. The distinction between the life, ministry and
death of Jesus and Christ risen must not be passed over by
contemporary Churches and theologians any more than it
was passed over by the first Churches and theologians who
gave us the synoptic Gospels. Paul's proper usage of the
Risen Christ as symbol for the Kingdom Jesus preached must
not mislead us into conflating Jesus-Kingdom-Christ with
the current Church(es) any more than it misled the communities which finally gave us the gospels of Matthew,
Mark and Luke. This warning should be printed in large
and bold type on all packets of Irish theology.

The move from the particular to the universal which 'Jesus
and the Kingdom' symbolises, takes its fuller form in personal-
social terms. The tendency in so much historical and more
recent theology to think of one's relationship with Jesus in
strictly individual personal terms (a more acute Protestant
temptation) or of any social dimension in strictly Church
terms (a more acute Catholic temptation, applicable also to

some left-wing reformation groups) must be corrected by the universal sweep of the Kingdom with its social and secular dimensions. The Kingdom is as broad as creation. Ecclesial as distinct from social, sacred as distinct from secular finally lose their significance in the fulfilment of the Kingdom. In its gradual realisation in history these distinctions are seriously relativised while remaining significant for a serving ecclesia that recognises the basic God-given and God-destined character of all that we call sacred and secular. In the language of our third and last critical Christian metaphor, the Church(es) serve the coming Kingdom by assisting at the re-birth of creation in new creation.

Creation and New Creation

In selecting critical Christian symbols or metaphors for the development of an Irish theology, or indeed of any theology, criteria are bound to be undeveloped, actual choices provisional and the process of choosing partly intuitive in the sense that it cannot be made fully explicit or justified beforehand. The first two metaphors — Exodus and Israel, Jesus and the Kingdom — have had certain obvious prior support in contemporary concern (Exodus and Liberation theology) or Christian tradition (Kingdom in Gospels and subsequently). Creation and New Creation do not command the same theological interest today and did not in evangelical times. Pauline development of the theme has never played more than a minor role in the subsequent tradition. Yet it may prove a particularly fruitful symbol in an age where the cosmos and history are more clearly intertwined in the great dramas of good versus evil, of destruction and even annihilation versus conservation, development and creativity. The nuclear threat to the human race and assorted threats to the world's ecological system increasingly display inner connexions. The growth of desert and infertile areas with continually increasing famine in Africa and elsewhere are related, at least in the inadequate response to them, to the structures of world trade and economies as the bloated West and North pile their granaries high and dig their milk and wine lakes deep ('Fool, this night your soul is required of you' Lk. 12 : 20). The role of the arms industry in the domestic economies of the USA, USSR, Britain, France and others, together with that of the international arms trade where 'aid' may be conditional on accepting particular kinds and amounts of weapons, emphasise again the shared fate of planet earth and human history. With creation threatened, through human stupidity, weakness, greed and power-seeking, by its very reversal in the annihilation of life and life's resources on earth, the summons and the power of new creation become particularly urgent.

In Christian history new creation comes by way of Calvary. The seed falling into the ground must itself die to issue in new life. The new Adam, new head of creation, is the risen Christ (Rom. 5). The whole cosmos is straining for that transformation of humanity, of earthly life, of earth (Rom. 8) which derives from 'a winter tree/Golden with fruit of a man's body' (R. S. Thomas).

The continuity and discontinuity between birth, death and re-birth characteristic of creation and all its living levels, is given new power and meaning with the birth, death and resurrection of Jesus Christ. New Creation is a deepening and transcending of the original gift/grace of Creation. Through the participation of the creating God even in the suffering of all creation's birth and dying, the apparently simple cycle is broken utterly and irreversibly. New creation, always the transcendent doppelgänger of creation, emerges in its true presence and power with the risen Christ. All that we in our authentic moments are and do and say, all that we cultivate into flourishing of the earth and of humankind carries the seed of eternity. Nothing of all this shall be lost. Adam's Curse (W. B. Yeats) by which 'It's certain that no fine thing/ since Adam's fall but needs much labouring' will always haunt us but the fine things are possible and have significance beyond the 'labouring' and 'the hours' required to make it seem but 'a moment's thought'. The artist who is our creator God (Gibson Winter) provides the enabling and enduring power to sustain us in all caring and creative activity that will reverence the potential of the given, that will opose its exploitation and destruction, and that will reveal and release the new creation of earth and humanity symbolised and realised in Jesus Christ. In an Ireland which has always combined a celebratory nature poetry with a penitential religion, a startingly beautiful geography with a destructive history, the passage from Creation to New Creation could be a particularly illuminating theological metaphor.

III. IRISH PARTICULARS, THEOLOGICAL METHODS AND METAPHORS

Social, political and cultural analysis of the context in which one seeks to do theology has entered much more explicitly into theological consciousness today. It was never entirely absent. Studies of the social background to Jesus' mission, which have been such a valuable feature of recent New Testament scholarship, help us to understand the limitations and possibilities confronting Jesus but there is no scholarly conclusion of which I am aware, that Jesus was unaware of these possibilities and limitations, that he failed to make his own social analysis, however implicitly and intuitively. Similar studies of Paul and early Church history reveal the complexities of the context and the reasons for certain responses but they are not blind or unexamined responses to an unexamined social and cultural situation. The more recent developments of historical consciousness and of social, political and economic as well as cultural analysis, have naturally led to a more self-conscious, self-critical approach to the theological task in any particular situation. The various methodological moves discussed earlier illustrate some of this new theological self-consciousness and self-criticism. Analysis, like historical study earlier, never takes just one form and may well in its theological employment repeat the exclusivist mistakes of, for example, positive historicism, based on too close analogy with what was taken to be the scientific method supreme — that of the physical sciences. The questioning of these very methods as true of the physical sciences must give all seekers after one, true, holy and catholic scientific method serious reason for rethinking their confusion of scientific (*wissenschaftlich*), rigorous and critical method with a particular positivist understanding of the method of the physical sciences.

In Ireland positivism in theological method was more influential than many of its practitioners realised, while the analogy with the sciences was seldom observed. The positivism derived from a post-Reformation approach to theology as apologetic explanation and defence of the doctrines of a particular Church and tradition, both Reformation and Counter-Reformation. In the one tradition the positivist study took the Bible as its starting-point; in the other it took Church teaching or doctrines. This of course is a simplification and in Assembly College, Belfast, Trinity College, Dublin and Maynooth, Presbyterian, Anglican and Catholic theologians were more comprehensive and sophisticated. Since Vatican II and what has been frequently called the end of the Counter-Reformation, a fresh liberation of theologians has occurred with crossing-over of starting-points, methods and criteria. Yet theologians of all Church traditions in Ireland are faced with an increasingly urgent task of understanding and presenting the Gospel message in a rapidly changing society. It is only in co-operation that they can hope to achieve the social analysis and theological response which the situation demands.

Religious Particulars

The analysis of the religious particulars of the Irish situation can never abstract from other features, cultural, social, political and economic. The obvious divisions between Churches vary with political setting and affiliation, social situation and economic conditions, cultural and educational background. These same variables apply to divisions within the Churches and not just between them. While Northern Protestants and Northern Catholics are sharply and sometimes bitterly divided on a host of religious and other issues, they may be closer together than either group is to its southern counterpart on certain things. The united Church front against the change on the laws of homosexuality in Northern Ireland would be difficult to replicate in the South. The unemployed of East (Protestant) and West (Catholic) Belfast may have a deeper unity in real religious belief or unbelief than their slogans suggest and share that unity with the unemployed in Finglas or Ballyfermot. Official Church affiliation and official Church statements do not necessarily reflect the real affiliation or beliefs of all Church members. The exploration and analysis of this complexity

116

demands greater attention from social scientists, theologians and pastors than it has hitherto received. Atheism and theism, agnosticism and ecuminism, Irish style, frequently lead hidden or disguised lives. Yet one has to start with what is more generally known and more evidently available for analysis.

In seeking to understand the particular Christian traditions in Ireland and their historical hostilities, the narrative takes precedence over the systematic. A non-historical comparison of the Decrees of the Council of Trent, the Thirty-Nine Articles and the Westminster Confession or of the more popular presentations of them in catechetical literature cannot do justice to the texts themselves; let alone to the communities which cherish them. These communities, reaching back to their origins in the New Testament and intervening Church history, with a history of four hundred years of living and adapting their Reformation and Counter-Reformation heritages, are not to be frozen in their beliefs and cannot be confined to one particular systematic textual expression of those beliefs without reference to the story/history in which these texts are formulated and accepted.

The narrative approach to the Irish Churches, their beliefs and theologies, may first of all heighten the misunderstanding and hostility as the wounding memories of recurring political, economic and cultural quarrels intrude into the religious story. Yet that is a necessary first step. Wounds were inflicted; they need to be exposed and accepted if they are to be healed. The fuller narrative context can help to understand the wounding as it can in retrospect and prospect confront the believing but divided communities with an older heritage and a future horizon that may reveal possibilities of convergence which the sixteenth-century religious freeze ignores. The common medieval tradition was more influential in Reformation renewal than is frequently acknowledged. Beyond that the Celtic Church itself has had its influence, directly and indirectly, on the major Irish Christian Churches. The Roman Catholic Church and Church of Ireland recognise this very directly in their honouring of Patrick and Columbanus. The less direct influences on the Scots-Irish Presbyterian tradition through the Celtic Church influence in Scotland could be more fully accepted. It may not be fanciful to suppose that the pentitential and near pessimistic strand in

117

pre-Reformation Irish and Celtic Christianity found congenial company in the Calvinism of John Knox. The Irish Penitentials and St Patrick's Purgatory are monuments to an older Celtic sense of sin. Beyond the peculiarly Celtic the patristic inheritance, above all St Augustine, has continuing influence on this sinful dimension of Irish Christianity. It would be unfair to exaggerate the sinful strand. Early Irish spirituality had a great sense of joy in creation and Creator. The development of Irish penance and penitential books took away some of the more painful features of public penance at the same time as a quite bawdy tradition of Irish literature with a religious background was emerging. All of this forms the story of an Irish Christianity that none of our Churches properly understands and accepts today.

The medieval, the Celtic and the patristic roots are finally planted in the soil of the New Testament. This is our glory story, the story of Jesus and of the first disciples or Church. Reading our separate Church stories through the earlier history eventually confronts us with our originating story in Jesus. How to let that confrontation with the New Testament form the basis of convergence for Churches divided in Ireland and elsewhere is a central task of the search for Church unity. In Ireland this confrontation for convergence could have the enormously liberating effect of releasing the Churches, of promoting their exodus from the Egypt of sixteenth-century religious and subsequent political, social and cultural confinement. The careful and prayerful referring of Irish Church stories along their divided and shared historical paths to the path and way of Jesus is a major task for Irish theologians, which will demand the critical ways of theology in its systematic and narrative modes, understood and applied ecumenically.

The prospect for the Christian future in Ireland faces the ultimate eschatological horizon of convergence which at once relativises our divisions and divided allegiances. At the same time it summons us to work urgently for Christian unity as sign and realisation of human unity, of the incoming Kingdom. The urgency of that work may not be ignored on the plea that full Christian and human unity lies beyond history. It is only through work in history, accepting and responding to the in-breaking, transforming and unifying God of Jesus

Christ in all his incarnate forms, that the eschatological unity is to be achieved and shared.

The penultimate human tasks and responsibilities enter into the ultimate divine gift and achievement. In Irish conditions signs and realisations of that task should relate to the still strong sense of Church, Church affiliation and Church attendance which most Irish Christians share. Church signs and realisations of the coming sign of the Kingdom have always been ambiguous in history. Taking the Churches back to the story of Jesus can renew their sense of responsibility for the Kingdom and their sense of failure in recognising and promoting it. Hostile Church affiliations, particularly in a society with active Church participation, constitute a counter-sign of the Kingdom and a betrayal of Jesus. Inter-Church liturgies of the Word, of baptism and of marriage can constitute important witness to the Kingdom in the Irish situation. So will the regular attendance at one another's Eucharistic celebrations. Theologians must fulfil their ecumenical vocation by exploring in the critical Irish situation the possibilities of shared Eucharist as expressing the unity achieved and promoting further unity. The current difficulties about inter-Church marriages which could and should be signs of the new ecumenical commitment to the Kingdom seem altogether out of proportion in these demanding times. The relation of Jesus to Kingdom with its consequent relativising and emphasising of Church as sign and instrument of Kingdom could indicate ways of inter-Church support for inter-Church marriages in seeking an agreed inter-Church form of education for the children. The present unseemly quarrel adds to the Churches' failures to be authentic witnesses to the saving presence of God in history.

Political, Social and Cultural Pressures

The role of narrative in understanding the entanglement of religion with political, social and cultural dimensions of Irish life seems self-evident. Some very significant work by Irish historians, North and South, has led to considerable convergence in the interpretation and presentation of 'secular' history. This has had an important influence in the schools although it is not so evident in political and other public

119

attitudes and activities. For the most part this history has ignored religious practices and interpretations except in so far as formal Church authorities were involved in directly political issues. Church historians and especially theologians must pay much more attention to the achievements of historians who usually see themselves as having primarily secular interests or who may lack the theological background or interest to go beyond the fair-minded and thorough record to any deeper analysis. A series of important studies on Church-State relations in Ireland from mid-nineteenth to late twentieth century has not received the theological attention they deserve.

At the same time the cultural and social dimensions of Irish life are being subjected to increasing critical study. Some of this study focuses on Irish religious and moral attitudes and behaviour and has obvious theological interest. A good deal more looks at wider economic and social practices and contains a more subtle challenge for Churches and theologians. Current renewal in the artistic and cultural life of the country, in literature of course, poetry, drama and fiction, but also in the visual and plastic arts, offers Church people and theologians insights into Irish life, frustrations and aspirations which they cannot afford to ignore.

In this brief survey of Irish pressures I must emphasise the economic conditions for two reasons. The first is that economic distress and chronic increasing unemployment constitute a major problem for our society. The developing division in Ireland as in so many other countries is between those who are accepted, included and participate in society because they have work and those who appear and feel rejected and excluded from society because they have no work. Given their age, skills and social background, many may never work again and indeed may never work at all. This exclusion with its alienating consequences (to use the fashionable word) must be socially destructive of individuals, even of whole groups and classes. In theological terms it exposes the obstacles to the Kingdom emerging in society as expressed by a united, sharing and participating people. In the wastage of human and communal resources it contradicts the creative dynamism of the God of Genesis and of the New Testament. Without a transformation that permits the movement from

120

Creation to New Creation, chaos in human lives and relation-ships will spread as the unemployed and excluded become disaffected and, even, destructive or — still worse — decline into apathy and disintegration.

Permanent and pervasive unemployment is a serious coun-tersign to the Kingdom. Its challenge to theology may be met to some extent by invoking the performative character and method of theology and the Gospel primacy it accords to the deprived. It is in the doing, the performing, the active solidar-ity with the unemployed, particularly the most deprived of these and the conventionally unemployable that the Churches in their faith-reflexion may be able to discern the true pres-ence and prior demands of the Kingdom. Without this per-formative dimension in Ireland, North and South, without attending to those excluded from working and so from shaping their own destiny and that of their society, much Church teaching and theologising will remain at best ineffec-tually abstract and irrelevant, and at worst a subtle and profound reinforcement of the status quo and of the place and power of the privileged. In either case the Gospel is being betrayed; idols of power and money are replacing the dis-ruptive God of Jesus Christ; the 'excluded' who will go first into the Kingdom stand in judgment over Church leaders and theologians. An Irish theology in service of the King-dom, which seeks to promote Creation and New Creation over chaos, will have to prove its worth in developing a per-formative method in solidarity with the Irish deprived.

CONCLUSION

The obvious conclusions to this chapter and to the book as a whole is that there is no one single, simple or even com-pletely coherent method of practising theology in an Irish context. A combination of methods will always be used. So will a combination of personal talents and training among theologians of different social and educational backgrounds and interests. Above all perhaps there is needed just now in Ireland a combination of ecclesial affiliations. Theology must be a communal enterprise drawing on the widest resources of the ecclesial communities to help preach, discern and promote the Kingdom in society. Such a communal enterprise must be clearly inter-Church. It must have lay as well as clerical believers. It must transcend the traditional exclusion of women as theologians. It must employ systematic and narrative methods in an idiom that reflects Jesus' engagement with the excluded as a way of promoting the final inclusivity of the Kingdom. That engagement implies a performative dimension to theology that must be liberating and creative for theology, the Churches, human society and planet earth.

Such a series of 'musts' sounds moralistic, even self-righteous in tone. The limited work of theologians would not justify any such high-and-mighty approach to their colleagues and their Churches. And indeed some of these demands have received at least an initial response from a variety of Church people, lay and clerical, professional and non-professional in the theological sense. The beginnings of the necessary Irish theological enterprise have emerged in Ballymurphy and Ballymun, in various institutions, in inter-church groups of quite different kinds. Its further development depends on the dedication, thoughtfulness and performance of a wider range of Irish Christians.

10.

Dying for the Cause:
An Irish Perspective on Martyrdom

The Irish Political Tradition

IN THE wake of the London bombings of 20 July 1982, in which ten soldiers died, responsible British politicians rejected the suggestion that the death penalty should be introduced for terrorists, partly on the grounds that it would provide the IRA with fresh 'martyrs'. The IRA hunger-strikers who died in 1981 were regarded by their followers and some outside observers as such political martyrs, dying to bear witness to the justice of their political cause. (I had this confirmed in discussion with Africans from South Africa in August 1982.) In all this, supporters and opponents of the present IRA campaign are very conscious of the explicit invocation of martyrdom, with all its sacred overtones, by the Irish political tradition to which the IRA proclaim allegiance. The Manchester 'martyrs' executed by the British in 1867 were a paradigm case. In the run-up to the next revolution in Easter 1916 the leaders set great store by the Fenian dead and their graves, like the early Christians honouring the martyrs and their tombs. Padraic Pearse, ultimately commander-in-chief of the revolutionary forces, spoke of the need for bloody self-sacrifice by the few to restore the self-respect and the spirit of Ireland. The execution of the 1916 leaders shortly after the collapse of the revolution did indeed reawaken the Irish drive for independence. The name and role of martyr continued to fuel that struggle for independence.

Some later commentators have expressed shock at the

appropriation by a secular political cause (Irish Nationalism) of the properly religious tradition of martyrdom and at the consequent confusion between nationalism and religion. The confusion has been compounded in Ireland (as elsewhere) by the close (but not entire) overlapping between religious and political traditions. In Ireland Nationalists, favouring Irish independence from Britain, have been mainly but not exclusively Catholic; Unionists, in favour of maintaining the union with Britain, have been dominantly Protestant. The martyrs and saints of the one side tend to be the enemies and demon-figures of the other; William of Orange and Sir Edward Carson on the Unionist side *v.* Wolfe Tone (Protestant) and Padraic Pearse on the Nationalist side.

Ireland is by no means unique in honouring political martyrs with a religious intensity, as it is not alone in the near coincidence of opposing political and religious traditions. Ireland's tangled history and the continuing destructive instability of Northern Ireland demand careful reflexion on the meaning and role of martyrdom as it emerged in Christian tradition, and developed in the history of the West. How far it already contained or subsequently acquired a political dimension; whether and when this political dimension became a dominant one; how far martyrdom entered into a people's self-definition or identity; and whether this identity, religious or political, became a closed and excluding identity issuing in idolatry: these are questions which a contemporary study of martyrdom must face. They are questions which the particular case-study of Ireland can partially illuminate, if not finally answer.

Martyrs in the Christian Tradition: Religious or Political?

The early Christian martyrs who shaped Christian praxis and theory of martyrdom, were consciously witnessing to Jesus Christ, to his Gospel, his person and his achievement. They saw themselves as followers and imitators willing to 'confess him before men', taking up their cross to follow him, following and imitating him even unto his death on a cross. His laying down of his life for his friends was their model and inspiration. His conflict with and execution by the religious and political establishment of his day was accepted as their

124

inevitable lot. They attempted to maintain continuity with Israel in temple and synagogue. Their proto-martyr Stephen and the presence at his death of arch-persecutor Saul exposed the deepening rift. More significant in space and time was the presence and power of the Empire to which they persistently proclaimed allegiance. It was a necessarily qualified allegiance to a necessarily relativised Empire. The Kingdom which Jesus had preached and to which Christians must be primarily loyal, was not indeed of this world in the sense of its being a historical, political alternative to the Empire or the other kingdoms of this world. Yet its proclamation and the allegiance it demanded relativise all human kingdoms. Membership of them could not exhaust the reality of citizens who were called to recognise the presence and power of the saving God of Jesus Christ in the incoming Kingdom which he had anounced and inaugurated. A historical kingdom which absolutised itself, which required worship of its gods as well as obedience to its laws, as the Roman Empire did, conflicted with the claim of one true God and his Kingdom. Christians realised that they had to obey God rather than men and their created deities or idols. The Roman Empire, like all political kingdoms, would now be relativised, radically diminished. To that threat the Empire reacted defensively, violently, in persecution of the Christians. Christian martyrs died bearing witness to the power and presence of God which Jesus embodied in himself and proclaimed as the Kingdom.

Without entering into the details of the debate of how far and in what way the mission and death of Jesus were precisely political for that time and place, one can say that his mission and death had the inevitable political effect of relativising and restraining all historical political enterprises. These might no longer make the absolute and divine claims advanced by the Roman Empire and repeated in frequently harsher terms by absolute or totalitarian regimes ever since. In maintaining and defending unto death the freedom to recognise and respond to their God, the early Christian opened up a permanent area of freedom for the person and revealed a permanent limitation of politics and the law. In this area of freedom and by recognition of this limitation of politics, the person is seen to transcend the citizen and what we now call human rights to transcend political authority and State law.

125

This is a critical and in principle irreversible political achievement initiated by Christianity and its early martyrs.

The achievement in principle was frequently obscured in practice once Christianity became part of the imperial establishment. This is illustrated by the switch in Augustine's attitude to the Donatists — first commitment to persuasion and free conversion and then to invoking the aid of the Roman council and appealing to the Scriptural text 'Compel them to come in'. The history of Christendom renders at best ambiguous evidence of the limitations on the political and of the freedom of the person to which the early martyrs bore witness. The death of Thomas à Becket, Archbishop of Canterbury, at the hands of Henry II shows how Christian witness survived in face of political claims. Too many episcopal colleagues of Becket, from Rome to Canterbury, were more ready to collaborate with and even encourage political rulers in activities that reflected absolute rather than relative claims over their subjects. This they demonstrated in conversion by the sword and in the execution of heretics as traitors. Such practices persisted long after the break-up of Christendom both in the new world and in the post-Reformation States. As the modern world was born, Christians, now belonging to different and opposing Churches, were long in disrepute as the defenders of persons against powers, as upholders of freedom, even religious freedom, except for that of their own denominational members. The potential for personal freedom and restraint on power which Christian martyrdom had expressed, was for the most part obscured by alliance with power in pursuit of Church privilege. The new champions of freedom were avowedly secular in origin and aim. Such champions included witness unto death for the new secular and political freedom heralded for example by the American and French revolutions.

In its dependent and oppressed tradition Ireland was influenced by the new freedom involvements. Theobald Wolfe Tone, father of Irish republicanism, was greatly influenced by Paine's *The Rights of Man* and strenuously sought to enlist the aid of the new French revolutionary government. The 1798 Irish revolution, despite its failure and that of the French expedition, and despite the death of Wolfe Tone in prison, initiated a new stage in the struggle for civil and political freedoms by oppressed Irish Catholics, and in the more radical movement for separation from England into an independent republic.

It is from the inevitable convergence of these two struggles for Catholic Emancipation and political independence that the present-day intertwining of Catholicism and Nationalism stems. It is from the more radical separatist republican tradition that the latter-day Irish political 'martyrs' have come. Have the secularising and relativising of politics by the early Christian martyrs given way to the resacralising and absolutising of them by the new political martyrs from Ireland and a host of other countries? Or is there a Christian sense to secular and political martyrdom of the kind experienced in Ireland?

Martyrdom and Identity: Question and Ambiguities

In the course of history Christian martyrs have presented the Church with opportunities and demands to identify itself as the community witnessing to the saving presence and power of God in the world, the Kingdom announced by and inaugurated in Jesus Christ. The need for such self-identification by the Church continues. The need for witnesses, even unto death, to question and relativise the powers of this world is no less real although the manner of such witness varies enormously. Unless the Church in its witness is questioning and exposing the absolute pretensions of political, economic and other contemporary powers, Jesus' Kingdom will continue to be obscured and obstructed. Where that witness is finally death-accepting in the cause, after the fashion and by the power of Jesus, the life-giving proclamation of the Gospel is renewed. Maximilian Kolbe, Dietrich Bonhoeffer, Martin Luther King and Oscar Romero encourage the hope of renewal for the current generations.

Yet historical and contemporary martyrdom raise a number of serious questions about the causes for which 'martyrs' die, the manner in which they meet their death and the effects which their deaths have on the communities to which they belong. Despite the apparently clear and clean historical record of the people we honour as Christian martyrs, ambiguities abound.

In so many ways in the history and theology of Christian martyrdom the cause has been crucial. This corresponds to the wider Christian tradition on life and death issues in which the 'just cause' in the case of war provides a characteristic example. The general point at issue here is the critical role of 'cause' in understanding and evaluating life and death issues for the Christian.

The identifying of the martyr's cause as Jesus' cause and the translation of that into witness to the Kingdom does not remove all the obscurities and ambiguities, as the different circumstances and causes of Justin Martyr and Maximilian Kolbe Martyr or the 'opposing' causes of Catholic and Protestant martyrs at the time of the Reformation readily reveal. An important continuity of cause recurs, I believe, and may be expressed as witness to God's Kingdom even when that takes on more apparently secular form in service and protection of the neighbour. Jesus ultimately witnessing to the Kingdom was Jesus laying down his life for his friends. Despite the obvious connection between Church community and Kingdom of God, Christian martyrs do not die solely, even primarily, for the sake of the Church community but for the Kingdom which may be seeking expression and demanding recognition outside the bounds of the historical Church, in causes not explicitly religious. So much the centrality of love of neighbour to the appearance and practice of the Kingdom should always tell us.

The broader reaches of love of neighbour clearly provide adequate cause for giving one's life. In the many oppressive situations in which one lives today that life-giving will have an immediately political rather than religious context as, in their different ways, Kolbe, Bonhoeffer, King and Romero discovered. Their and others' recognition as Christian martyrs, as witnesses unto death to the truth and grace of God's Kingdom, will reflect their own and the Christian community's understanding of their enterprise, dying for their friends in the manner and by the power of Jesus Christ.

It would be foolish to resist extending the range of Christian martyrdom, then, to those who give their lives for their neighbour in political contexts. It would be equally foolish to interpret all deaths for political causes as even ambiguous instances of Christian martyrdom.

The understanding of the people themselves and of the Christian community is relevant to the recognition of martyrs, but the prior, more objective, criterion of the cause as some inbreaking of the Kingdom is not always easily applicable. The opposing political options for Northern Ireland illustrate the difficulty of identifying political causes as Christian causes to which one might bear witness with one's life. There is, however, some further guidance available on the appropriateness of the cause as one reflects on its effects, particularly the relationship between martyrdom and identification.

The self-identification of a community by its appeal to its 'martyrs' does not apply exclusively to religious communities. The invocation of Fenian graves by leaders of the Irish revolution has already been quoted as a political instance. The Irish conflict clearly involves a conflict of identities nurtured by the memory of martyrs in conflict.

A critical Christian question for such community identification and its martyr support, is how far a fresh human absolute has emerged. How far, in the Irish instance, is the supreme determinant of allegiance and behaviour, membership of a United Ireland or of the United Kingdom? Does some national political ideal override all other consideration, including considerations of life and death? Has the ideal become an idol to which we surrender all that we are and have, including our sense of the relativity of all such ideals in the face of God's kingdom? Have we found a substitute God, an alternative supreme being, more properly described in that telling term as a godling? A test of where our final allegiance lies will continue to be, what are we prepared to die for? A more frightening one may be, what are we prepared to kill for? And pressing that test further we ask how far the ideal is pursued at the expense of the people? How far the 'what' has replaced the 'who' in the evaluation of our killing and dying?

That is not intended as a complete evaluation of killing or dying for political causes. It is calling attention to how these causes may be absolutised and how that absolutising involves the relativising of people, even whole races or generations as we have experienced in this century. Such absolutising is the antithesis rather than the expression of the Kingdom and dying for it does not fit the pattern of Christian martyrdom.

Political leaders are not the only people exposed to the temptations of absolutising. Political ideals and the power centred about them are not the only ones which take on the mantle of idol. Church leaders and Church power may yield to the same temptations. And killing in the name of Church or Jesus as evidenced in the Crusades and frequently invoked to bless subsequent wars, offers an important clue to the failure of the Church to see itself as limited embodiment and servant of the Kingdom but not identical with it.

All this may not be taken as an excuse to ignore the justice and urgency of particular causes or the obligation to enter the struggle for them as deriving from our Kingdom commitment. Indeed it may not be taken to exclude the need to fight for them by means of physical force in particular circumstances. It does, however, call attention to the ambiguities of such causes, the dangers that they may easily be absolutised, how this danger may be enhanced by the appeal to martyrs and how this absolutising easily leads to killing rather than dying for one's cause. One should be very circumspect therefore in using the name 'martyr', restricting it as far as possible to where somebody clearly sacrificed him or herself to maintain or achieve justice for others, a clearly Kingdom cause.

Victims and Martyrs

The others constitute the primary test of all genuine self-sacrifice, the others in their needs, in their privations and oppressions, the others as victims. Victimhood and martyrdom are intimately connected. All martyrs are victims, victims of human powers pretending to absoluteness. But are all victims martyrs? Are all the millions of victims of historical powers we have known even in this century to be classified as martyrs, dying for the Kingdom, however implicitly? Perhaps many more are than we have previously recognised, their witness lost on us. Yet some distinction between martyr and victim may be necessary to preserve the traditional force of martyrdom without letting us lapse

130

once again into the forgetfulness of the victims which remains such a disturbing feature of human consciousness, including that of Christians.

The witness of Jesus was expressed in his victimhood. The victim of Calvary, on one important reading, was carrying to its conclusion his identification of himself and his God with the victims of the society in which he lived. By siding with them, attending to them, identifying with them he took on their victimhood, he accepted human victimhood itself. That acceptance and its expression on Calvary may be understood as the victimhood to end all victimhood as it was the sacrifice to end all sacrifices. In Jesus' death and resurrection victimhood was taken on fully, and finally overcome. He was the victim to end all victims. The Kingdom he proclaimed excluded victimhood. The humble and lowly would be raised from their oppression. The prisoners would be set free. Victims of physical illness would be healed. The poor, the general category of victims, were to receive this good news (Lk. 4). Calvary revealed the last victim as prelude to the new life and freedom, peace and justice of the Kingdom.

Yet victimhood goes on. The followers of Jesus are at once puzzled and challenged. Why hasn't the Kingdom come? the puzzle. What is our obligation to let it come? the challenge. We must recognise the problems of the puzzle but refuse to be paralysed by it as we take up the challenge — the challenge to remove victimhood, to witness to the coming of the Kingdom by opposing and seeking to remove the diverse oppressions which continue to obscure and obstruct the Kingdom by creating and maintaining victims. It is in taking on victimhood, by identifying with the victims and struggling for their release that we bear witness to the Kingdom. We may do that from a position initially free from the particular condition of the victims, by entering into that condition and seeking to change it. We may seek to do this as victims already enmeshed in that condition and by opposing and seeking to change the conditions, bear witness to and promote the Kingdom which excludes victimhood. In opposing the oppressive powers on behalf of the (other) victims we follow Jesus to his bitter end. In giving our lives in such a cause we properly merit the title and honour of martyr, witness unto death to the presence and power of the Kingdom.

131

Martyrs are victims. They share the conditions of victims and by opposing endure the final victimhood of Calvary. They remind Christians of the prevalence and depth of human victimhood and challenge them to oppose in turn. They remind them of the contemporary Calvaries which crowd the world. They seek to live the prayer 'Thy Kingdom come' by seeking to remove the victim conditions of the neighbour even at the price of ultimate victimhood.

The coming of the Kingdom in history and politics is a summons to Christians. One way to test its concrete demands is to ask: who are the victims? One way to make a concrete response is by accepting the cause of the victims. The martyr recognises that response as 'costing not less than everything' (Eliot).

11.

Northern Ireland:
The Need for Double Vision

THE ANGLO-IRISH Agreement signed by the British and Irish governments in November 1985 was hailed by many in Britain and Ireland as the solution to our problems, although its architects more properly presented it as a critical step forward in a process that would lead to a solution. Unionist opposition has made even that modest claim questionable and the future effectiveness of the Agreement is by no means assured. One of its guiding principles was an attempt to do justice to the two-fold interests and responsibilities of Britain and the Republic of Ireland and to the two-fold identities and aspirations of the communities in Northern Ireland. Such double vision will always be necessary to a just and stable solution.

In this chapter I rehearse some arguments for double vision by British and Irish, Protestant and Catholic. The arguments were developed some time before the Agreement but the analysis remains, I believe, valid and pertinent, whatever the immediate fate of the Agreement.

I. BRITISH RESPONSIBILITY

British-Irish Problems

What follows was first composed as a lecture, at the request of the British audience before whom it was given. Speaking to an Irish audience the idiom and emphasis must be different. Indeed one of the difficulties in this as in every other complex situation is how to address different audiences and constituencies in ways that are accessible to them, honest to oneself and consistent with one another. The difference in idiom and emphasis can easily lead to charges of dishonesty and inconsistency. Attempts to use exactly the same language and approach with Unionists and Nationalists, British and Irish will undoubtedly leave one or other audience either completely untouched or moving between misunderstanding and hostility. It may help to remember that our close involvement with one another in these islands means that the complexity and divisions are reflected, though usually obscurely and wearily, in ourselves as individuals. History and geography, political structures and practices, languages (Celtic as well as Anglo-Saxon) and literatures, cultures and customs, media, migration and intermarriage are so interconnected that the peoples of Britain and Ireland, as communities, as persons, overlap and intertwine despite all the undoubted differences. The aspirations and frustrations of the Nationalists, the insecurity and need to retain power of the Unionists, the impatience and indifference of the British, to list some simple considerations, come together in varying degrees in the coalition which constitutes each of us. Elements of this coalition may be more or less dominant in individuals and groups. Other elements may be ignored or suppressed. Honest communication and developing community require of all of us in Britain and Ireland that the ignored or suppressed elements in our individual coalition are recognised and respected. Such a view of the internal complexity of the individual or the group, Unionist or Nationalist, Irish or British, does not of course dissolve basic identities or prevailing allegiances but it does qualify and, more importantly, enrich them.

Northern Ireland is a British-Irish problem. Too much discussion by people, politicians and media in Britain still gives the impression that it is an *Irish* problem. In the space of ten minutes on BBC one day I heard a reference to 'Irish terrorists' in relation to some bomb-incident, followed by a reference to the 'British' poet, Seamus Heaney. The terrorism is Irish but the poetry, like the athletic achievements of Mary Peters, is British. The widely diffused British line that they were holding the ring between two fighting Irish communities was dishonest in itself and seriously preventive of effective understanding and response. I sometimes anticipated these diffi-

134

culties by asking my British friends: 'How is the civil war going in your country?'

'Which war?' or 'Which country?' reflected their puzzled response.

'The war in the United Kingdom of course which, by the way, because you seem unable or unwilling to settle it, is costing my country, the Irish Republic, an enormous amount in security costs (three times as much per head of population as in the United Kingdom), in lost tourist revenue and lost investment, in reduced prestige abroad and reduced confidence at home.'

British evasion, which has frequently occurred, may easily be matched by Irish evasion. In reality this is a joint problem, if problem be not far too limited a term. And it is also a problem of joint suffering, suffering that is concentrated in the north eastern corner of the island of Ireland but involves both island peoples in death and destruction, impoverishment and fear. The overcoming of such destructive forces is the task of politics. This is ultimately an appeal to politicians for sustained political interest and action in the spirit of the attempt at the Anglo-Irish agreement. However it is an indirect appeal by way of the believing communities of the Churches. The basis of any appeal to the believing communities must be their belief, their faith in the God of Jesus Christ. The attempt to found that appeal in faith is a theological exercise.

Faith and Politics

Faith-reflexion on politics or theological analysis of politics is very much in fashion just now. One of the earlier, more provocative and profound remarks on this reflexion was that of American theologian Paul Lehmann when he spoke of the duty of Christians to discern what God was doing in the world and described that as politics. The recovery of the political dimension of faith and theology associated with the European school of Political Theology and the Latin American school of Liberation Theology has sharpened and developed our Christian understanding and commitment to the political task. Against that background there is a continuing need to provide faith-reflexion for Christians on Northern Ireland

135

suffering and the British-Irish responsibility. This is one more effort in that direction.

One of the most important lessons of the Latin American Liberation Theology movement is that theology must be localised or, as it goes in the trade, contextualised. Good theology (faith reflexion) arises out of particular situations to meet particular needs. The imperialism of central European theology has finally shattered. Particularity not universality becomes primary. This alone should be sufficient to warn us against the easy transfer of models of doing theology elsewhere into our own situation. For too long, theology, and especially Catholic theology in these islands, has lived by proxy, by importing uncritically the theological achievements of other times and places. The interdependence of all believing communities, past and present, and of their theological reflexion demands interchange but in a more critical and creative spirit. The developments in liberation and other theologies can help out but not substitute for our own attempts in our own situation.

Liberation Theology for Nothern Ireland?

For all the power of the Christian symbol of liberation with its Jesus-like commitment to the excluded and oppressed, it may not be the most helpful in seeking to discern what God is doing and demanding of British and Irish believers in relation to the tragedy of Northern Ireland. Our situation has its own peculiar characteristics which distinguish it markedly from Latin America and other places where the liberation symbol has been invoked so fruitfully. Of course oppression, including economic oppression, affects people in Northern Ireland as it does in South America. But there are at least two important distinguishing and complicating factors. These are in particular the conflicts of religious allegiance and of national identity with their close and reinforcing influence on each other. While it remains true that both communities in Northern Ireland and their 'parent' communities in Britain and the Republic of Ireland require, in Christian terms, liberation *from* and *to* one another, that very phrase in its complexity of 'from' and 'to' suggests the need for other, equally Christian and potentially more enriching symbols than liberation.

136

'Liberation' is one of the great Christian words and symbols, particularly apt to describe in general what God is doing in his world. It has received considerable attention over the last fifteen years. Equally biblical and theological words such as salvation, redemption and reconciliation reflect the same basic divine-human activity from other angles. Any or all of them could illuminate the particular difficulties, tasks and resources facing Christians in the challenge which Northern Ireland poses for Britain and Ireland. I prefer however to employ a different set of biblical terms, creation and new creation, in seeking to illuminate in faith these tasks and resources.

Creation and New Creation: General Symbol

In some theological discussions these terms are treated quite separately in an unrelated way. Creation has always been a subject of considerable theological attention while new creation rarely merited more than a passing mention in the treatment of redemption/salvation. (Reconciliation and liberation, prior to Liberation Theology, were treated with equal disregard). Creation was regarded predominantly as a once-for-all event and in the natural order. The continuing character more recently attributed to revelation, for exampled, did not affect the theology of creation to the same extent. Despite theology's move beyond the two-storied image and language of nature and supernature, creation, certainly in its sub-human dimensions, was for the most part seen as outside the ambit of grace, revelation, salvation and so in sharp contrast with new creation. The work of Teilhard de Chardin, his influence on Vatican II's *The Church in the Modern World*, the concern for ecology and the return to some of the great Pauline themes (cf. Michael Neary, 'Creation and Pauline Soteriology', *Irish Theological Quarterly*, 1983/4, n. 1), have helped to restore creation as a central and continuing reality in theological understanding. All this has prepared the way for fruitful connection with new creation in illuminating problems like those of destruction of the environment, the threat of nuclear holocaust and the more restricted, but deeply painful, conflict in Northern Ireland.

In discerning what God is doing in the world, creation,

as continuing divine activity, provides the first crucial image. The movement of the spirit over the waters, the gradual ordering and harnessing of the forces of the world symbolised in the overcoming of disorder or chaos, prepare the way for the emergence of living beings and finally of human beings, created in the image of God and enjoying divine familiarity. Of course the people of Israel did not experience the world in that harmonious and fruitful way. The chaos persisted in the uncontrollable waters and unyielding earth, in the danger from asp and lion, above all in the threat from stranger, neighbour and even brother, so powerfully illustrated in the Cain and Abel story. The creator God, Yahweh/Elohim, was needed to deal with this continuing chaos, to overcome it. He was not lacking in initiative and commitment as the great Mosaic covenant and its shadowy predecessors, reaching back through Abraham and Noah to *the* man, the first man, Adam, revealed. That initiative and commitment were to a fresh and continuing creative activity, to save his people and his world, to a new creation. The true depth and character of that divine involvement only became clear with Jesus of Nazareth, or rather after Jesus of Nazareth. After his death and new life in resurrection, the new creation was irrevocably established. The chaos of nature and humanity had done its worst, last of all to his own son, and had finally failed. Jesus was alive, raised to life by the God he called Father and invites and enables us to call Father.

The Persistence of Chaos

It's the great success story. Or is it? What about the centuries of persecution by the Romans? The chaos persisted. It took a more devastating turn with persecution and sword-point conversions of pagans by the Christians. And the inter-Christian wars — Christian killing Christian in the name of Jesus Christ a tradition still healthy and well and living in Northern Ireland? Beyond that little plot of land, the chaos goes on in wars and rumours of wars, rumours of the war not to end war but to end creation, nuclear war. Millions suffer starvation and thirst and other millions suffer the consequences of over-eating and over-drinking. The very fabric of land and sea is being unravelled by the thoughtless, hasty, greedy exploitation

138

of humankind. Has the chaos had its revenge? Did Jesus die in vain? Is the creative power of God unable to sustain the breakthrough from Calvary to Easter Sunday? Must the people of Northern Ireland and of these islands abandon hope of any end to their carnage and chaos?

God-suffering-with

In seeking to make sense of creation and new creation in the face of continuing chaos, we must return to the Jewish-Christian tradition to learn a little more of this creative God and his involvement with his creation. It is, as was indicated above, a continuing creative involvement. This continuing creative involvement passed through several stages in the history of Israel. A significant aspect of those stages was God's growing identification with his people. 'I shall be your God and you shall be my people' (Ex. 17). This identification of Israel in its enslavement in Egypt and subsequent history took Israel back eventually to God as creator, with the world reflecting God's goodness and glory, and the human being God's image, partner and friend.

In Israel's actual experience of Sin — Fall — Chaos, the divine commitment offered both judgment and empowerment or liberation, continuing creative activity in face of the chaos. In this activity human partners/friends were called to cooperate, to co-create. Failure was frequent and the consequent suffering enormous. Some of Israel's seers and prophets began to discern a new form of overcoming the chaos, a new form of creation, a new role for creator and co-creators. The suffering servant of Deutero-Isaiah prepared in some way for the extraordinary emergence of the suffering God in Jesus Christ. Israel itself in its various oppressions and exiles appealed for and was assured of the presence of the compassionate, the 'co-suffering' God. The divine strategy for overcoming the evil and chaos in the world became with Jesus a full entry into the human condition in a world caught between chaos and creativity, sin and grace, suffering and fullness of life. The incarnation of the Son of God was the critical symbol of this which then had to be followed through by taking on to the full the very chaos, destruction and suffering of humanity. The compassionate, 'suffering-with'

139

God manifested the depth of divine love and the radical source of new creation by taking on the chaos at its roots in the rejection, desertion, torture and execution of Jesus. Through this submission to final chaos came the definitive triumph of creativity, not as an immediately and completely achieved and recognisable 'Kingdom', but as a source, a way and an assurance. God's entry in Jesus into our sufferings and chaos has shown how divine creative power prevails and how we are to share in that power and prevailing by following Jesus' way. Our status as images of God, as co-creators stands more fully revealed in our sharing with God in the sufferings of all, so that we may share in the triumph over chaos in new creation.

The vision of God suffering with us, so strongly indicated in the Jewish-Christian tradition, has been greatly obscured by certain interpretations of the Greek tradition of a remote, unchangeable and impassible God. However we sort out the difficulty intellectually, and it will not be easy, we may not ignore the evidence and understanding of our tradition, that God shared with suffering humanity the impact of the chaos within us, between us and outside us. The attempts by process theologians to make some sense of such divine involvement with the world is an honourable try which should spur other theologians to further work.

In situations such as Northern Ireland, then, we can properly speak of God suffering with his people. And they are all his people, Protestant and Catholic, Unionist and Nationalist, British Army, U.D.R., U.D.A. and I.R.A. The sufferings of each individual and each group is shared by the incarnate, suffering God. The mutual infliction of suffering is a self-inflicted wound on oneself and one's compassionate God. The God of Jesus Christ is vulnerable to the chaos we cause and promote in our hostilities, injustices and wars. He is invaded and inhabited by these sufferings and this chaos so that he may overcome them in surrendering to them. The powerlessness of the suffering God so sharply highlighted by the Christian associations of British-Irish, Protestant-Catholic divisions becomes itself the very source of power. Calvary is complete only in Resurrection. But when is Calvary complete? How can one measure the three hours on the Cross in Northern Irish time? And when may the saving and healing power of God who assumes powerlessness be expected to break through to new life and new creation?

Christian Call to Suffer-with God in Northern Ireland

For the breakthrough we must be prepared. Going before him into Galilee means in this case, I believe, following the very way of God in Jesus. This can happen very dramatically as one reads some compelling account of human tragedy such as Elie Wiesel's account of the Holocaust in *Night* or as one watches on television starving women and children struggling over the Mozambique border into a Zimbabwe which is not able to support them either. Such dramatic, intense experience releases in us that image of God (creation) and sisterhood/ brotherhood of Jesus Christ (new creation) whereby we too can be inhabited by the suffering others, enter into their Calvary and so hope to share their and Jesus' resurrection. To be vulnerable to and inhabited by the sufferings of the others is to follow in the way of Jesus, to accept his Cross and the only way to resurrection. To expect any new life and new creation in our relationships in these island while we are closed to one another's sufferings is to be presumptuous Christians or simply unbelievers. As would-be Christians we Irish must be open to one another's sufferings in the different traditions, with Nationalist or Catholic open to the fears and sufferings of Protestants or Unionists. To us Catholics it may easily appear that the privations and oppressions of the minority community over the past sixty years far exceed those of the majority and are at least in part the responsibility of the majority. How then can we be expected to recognise, share, be inhabited by their sufferings? The overall oppression and suffering of the Northern minority is undeniable. Yet the very real sufferings and fears of the majority, which partly account for their treatment of the minority, may not be denied or ignored. Of course both sides suffer quite differently at different levels. From East Belfast to Malone Road to West Belfast the gap may be at least as wide as that between Unionists and Nationalists. But Protestant Unionists in general have real fears of their Catholic Nationalist neighbours in Northern Ireland and the Republic. They feel that unlike the Nationalists who are finally respected by the

141

Republic, they are not respected by any side and least of all by the British to whom they affirm such fervent loyalty and on whom they so sorely depend. We of the Irish Nationalist tradition who are Catholic must be open to these real sufferings of Unionists and Protestants just as they must be open to ours. In an Irish context I would want to develop this much further. My present concern is primarily with British responsibility.

Without a real sense of Irish suffering British Christians or politicians are never going to understand the depth and difficulty of our common problems. It is not, to begin with anyway, a matter of apportioning blame but of recognising British power and so British responsibility and so the need to understand. Without sharing the sufferings, being inhabited by them, understanding will not come. Neither will the commitment and capacity to help resolve it, to help overcome the chaos which is at least partly of British origin and British sustenance. Such openness to Irish suffering is a particular responsibility of British Christians. (The Irish openness to British suffering is also of course part of the overall picture.) Inhabited by the privations and fears and destruction of their closest neighbours, of people who share their very political structure in the United Kingdom, British Christians must give a lead in awakening the larger British public and their political leaders to an understanding and commitment which will prepare more effectively for the new creation which our God, who has entered the chaos, is calling for from the Cross. The current concern among Christians with a preferential option for the poor finds its final theological justification in God's identification with, being inhabited by, the poor, the suffering and the victims, and his summons to us to share, be inhabited by and so help alleviate and eventually overcome this suffering. In British-Irish relations, by entering into the suffering of both sides, God is calling each side to share the sufferings of the others in order to release his creative and saving power. With that kind of understanding and involvement, British Christians could and should ensure that the Northern Ireland problem be kept at the top of the political agenda in Britain.

This move by British Christians ought to be inter-Church for faith reasons. With my limited experience I find it simply impossible to think of engaging in such activities, such creative activities about Northern Ireland, such activities against the chaos, separately from those people who accept the same creator God of Jesus Christ. I would find it now really astonishing that I would be doing just my Catholic thing and they would be doing just their Anglican thing or their Presbyterian thing. Given a God-who-suffers-with, our divisions in the face of the struggle between creation and chaos in the world put us on the side of chaos. It is an act of unfaith contrary to the creator God.

Great problems remain which I can barely address. What about the power and what about the violence? We think of God as all-powerful and that, in a way, is what prevented us from thinking of him as suffering with us, until we had to be faced with Israel and the suffering servant and Jesus. We think that he properly subverted the power, the Powers of this world, and that some new concept of power emerged and it was a concept that was creative or enabling. We are therefore, talking about political structures that are enabling and not disabling of the people; that allow for their creative flourishing in different ways, for their traditions, communities. Not that their traditions and their personalities won't have destructive elements which will need to be overcome, but without an enabling, creative approach to power these will not be overcome. Part of this has been expressed in the political tradition in terms of 'freedom'. The significance of freedom and the great concern expressed at the erosion of civil liberties both here and in Northern Ireland indicate a disabling exercise of power, although some restraint of people who are themselves *simply* destructive and disabling is essential to the survival of freedom. The British record in Northern Ireland from 1920-1985 with the brief exception of Sunningdale and the Power-Sharing Executive, has been either disabling through lack of interest or disabling by giving simple priority to Law and Order. The Agreement of November 1985 offers fresh hope.

If the political power refuses sustained creative activity

and depends on delegation to a repressive group or insists again that Law and Order is all that matters, then, of course, it will evoke a chaotic response. Not that resistance is necessarily chaotic and not that, in history as we have known it, armed struggle hasn't been, at times, the way to creative achievement. It would seem to me, at this time in the century, in this particular context in Western Europe and with these responsibilities on us as Christians, that a more creative response is demanded. The suffering God is also a resisting God. He is a God who enables us to resist Evil; he resists it with us and as we endure and resist we may hope to transform and re-create. There does, again, seem to be a particular responsibility on the Churches to help find ways of creative expression of resistance, and creative ways of maintaining order. This does not mean that the non-violent option is primarily for the oppressed, if one were to use that term, or for the powerless and that that is the way they ought to go as Christians. We have to get our governments, the people with the responsibility for creating an enabling society, to look to non-violent ways of creating the peace and not just keeping the lid on. What I have been struggling with is how people in the island of Britain might discern what God is doing in the very difficult situation that confronts them; what he is summoning them to do and what he is finally empowering them to do.

II. IRISH RESPONSIBILITY

The great merits of Pádraig O'Malley's work *Uncivil Wars* (Blackstaff 1983) is its honest pursuit of objections to the positions on Northern Ireland taken by all political participants in Ireland and Britain. I discussed earlier some aspects of British responsibility in Northern Ireland. O'Malley's ruthless questioning of Irish positions raises important questions of Irish responsibility. Given the urgency of his objections to all current Irish positions, North and South, Unionist and Nationalist, there seems no prospect of progress or even of any authentic dialogue. O'Malley, despite his concern to move beyond the positions he so effectively undermines, does not offer any great reason for hope. He seems — rather like Robert Kee at the end of his television series,

Ireland, A Television History — to turn his back and walk away from the whole sorry mess. That this is not O'Malley's personal stance is clear from his continuing efforts to promote mutual understanding and dialogue. It did, however, seem to be the dominant message of his book. Something of the same critique of Nationalist positions emerges in Dervla Murphy's *Changing the Problem: Post Forum Reflections.* The report by the Inter-Church Group on Faith and Politics, *Breaking down the Enmity* offers independent but converging analysis although it opts for interim, internal moves as necessary and possible.

In presenting the difficulties so forcefully O'Malley, Murphy and the others challenge those who remain trapped by that destructive residue of British-Irish history now concentrated in Northern Ireland. To speak of it as a residue of history is not necessarily to engage in blaming anybody for the sins of forefathers. It is simply to recognise the origins of the problem and the continuing historical influences which any attempt of resolving it must confront. When an Irish commentator from the Republic speaks of history in this context he is frequently interpreted as simply condemning the British and the Unionists for the past and making a one-sided demand on them for the future. Such are the difficulties of speaking to different constituencies on this issue as discussed above. To acknowledge the force of history and the division of responsibility across the Irish Sea, is not to presume on how responsibility, past, present or future, is to be shared. In any case the primary concern here is with Irish responsibility and how Irish people may help one another to escape from the culs-de-sac into which certain widely-defended versions of their views can lead them.

The Churches and Northern Ireland

The involvement of religion and of the Churches in closing off political escape routes for Unionist and Nationalist is presented in oversimplified form by O'Malley, based perhaps on the dramatic needs of his account. The contribution of the Churches to maintaining communication and promoting harmony as charted, for example, in *Christmas in Ulster, 1969-1980* (Eric Gallagher and Stanley Worrall) is more significant than is frequently acknowledged by political

145

commentators or politicians. For all that, the Churches stand under judgment as the Inter-Church Group's report admits. The Churches cannot escape responsibility for political problems with which they are so intimately connected in origin and in maintenance. Political solutions certainly do not lie within Church leaders' competence. Whatever their will or know-how they simply lack the political power to alter political structures and achieve political peace.

Reinforcing or changing attitudes is, however, part of the Churches' political role. In Ireland inter-Church relations have frequently reflected and reinforced inherited and divisive political attitudes and so added to the sense of no alternative, no escape. Recent inter-Church developments need to go much further if they are to have adequate liberating social and political effects, if they are to create the space, as the football commentators say, within which the political players will have freedom of movement. That kind of inter-Church contribution to the British-Irish problem in Northern Ireland is not a matter exclusively for the Irish Churches, although theirs should be the more significant contribution.

How the Irish (and British) Churches may provide that space and promote that liberation will, I hope, emerge later. The strategy of this analysis employs language and methods characteristically associated with religion, particularly that of Israel, to probe the apparently closed-off positions of Irish politicians on Northern Ireland and the associated Church positions. The language will be that frequently used in Old Testament study but with adaptations at least applicable to politics. The substance will be mainly political, in its usual secular meaning. Yet language and substance will have obvious implications for the Churches and their role in the liberation of politics, a more urgent requirement in Northern Ireland than the politics of liberation.

The Priestly, Wisdom and Prophetic Traditions

Without entering into various scholarly debates about literary traditions in Old Testament writing and teaching, three traditions, the priestly, the wisdom and the prophetic, are relevant to our purposes. The three are not mutually exclusive or exhaustive as a description of Old Testament writings.

However, together they cover central aspects of the historical roles and writings of believing Israelites and they are sufficiently distinct to illuminate very different facets of these roles and writings.

The priestly tradition emphasises the worship dimension of human living with stress on the sacral or divine. Socially it tends to promote continuity with the great persons and achievements of the past and to fulfil an integrating and unifying role. This is typical of the Book of Deuteronomy in the Pentateuch and of particular traditions within other Pentateuch works, for example, the Book of Genesis.

The wisdom tradition has a more pragmatic, practical and therefore open attitude. In modern terms this is a more dialogical or ecumenical spirit. It enters into dialogue with other traditions. From the point of view of the strictly religious tradition it takes seriously insights from other traditions — both religious and secular. The Book of Proverbs reflects these pragmatic and open attitudes.

The third dimension of the tradition of Israel of immediate concern to us is the prophetic. Like the priestly, the prophetic is fiercely concerned with origins but in their roots or *radices* so that it can envisage quite new fruits in sympathy with the openness of the wisdom tradition. The new, however, is at once a fulfilment and transformation of the old so that the prophet can be sharply critical both of superficial conservative cherishing of the familiar and of superficial liberal openness to the novel. In the Hebrew tradition the creator God, of origins, always faithful to his covenant, is also the God of promise, ready to do a new thing, to take a new initiative, to make all things new. The major prophetic collections of Isaiah, Ezechiel and Jeremiah offer excellent examples of all this.

The God of Israel, of the Covenant, with his priestly demands of worship and fidelity, is also the God of all people. To him all must come and in the diverse ways of wisdom all now seek him. He is finally the God of renewal, of re-creation, of prophecy and transformation. For Christians Jesus as priest, king (wisdom figure) and prophet is the definitive revelation of this threefold way of God in continuity, openness and transformation.

The truths of Christianity (and of Judaism) are bound up with the discernment of God in creation and human history, of the divine in the human. The priestly, wisdom and prophetic strands in salvation history of both Jewish and Christian communities reveal at a deeper level dimensions of all human history and community. This illumination applies to the history of Britain and Ireland and that stage in the history of both which has issued in the apparently insoluble opposition of Unionist and Nationalist in Northern Ireland.

Within the Jewish tradition a critical combination of priestly, conserving concern with its powerful sense of past achievement, of wisdom with its dialogical openness to current and wider gifts, and of prophetic energy and insight directed at transforming the present, led Israel from Egypt to Sinai and the land of Canaan. Later Israel was opened up to the need and promise of a new covenant by a similar convergence of this threefold energy. For Christians the triple alliance issued in the life, death and resurrection of Jesus. For him the priestly past was so sacred that not one jot or tittle should be lost but all be fulfilled (Mt. 5:18). His openness to people beyond the priestly-defined limits, people like Samaritans, tax-collectors and prostitutes, was a notorious source of scandal. In the gospels wisdom-teaching characterises much that is central to the Christian way of life as illustrated in the Sermon on the Mount (with its quotations from Isaiah, Proverbs, Psalms and Wisdom). In this spirit of wisdom and openness Paul seeks to become all things to all men, a Jew to the Jews and a Gentile to the Gentiles (1 Cor. 9:11-27).

The prophetic energy of Jesus issued in a recall to the one true God of Israel and his mighty deeds but it resulted in the terrible and astonishing transformation of Calvary and Resurrection. So there is a new Moses, a new Adam, a new Israel, a new humanity and a new creation. The radically new has emerged by the seed falling into the ground and dying into new life. The deepest rhythms of human growth and change are mirrored in the life, death and resurrection of Jesus Christ. Continuity combines with discontinuity in revolution and fidelity. The dialectic applies across the range of human beings, relations, structures and achievements, as proper to created and creative sinful and redeemed humans. For Christians the energy and grace of priestly fidelity, wisdom openness and prophetic transformation apply to individuals and groups, to personal and social relations and structures in their secular as well as their religious dimensions.

Priestly, Wisdom and Prophetic in Northern Ireland's Politics

Within Northern Ireland and Ireland generally, the opposing secular and political traditions, Nationalist and Unionist, have their priestly, wisdom and prophetic strands. In many ways the prophetic is originating, centring on critical and revolutionary figures and events. For Unionists, William, the Battle of the Boyne, the Apprentice Boys of Derry from the seventeenth century connect with Carson, the Ulster covenant and the Larne gun-running in the early twentieth to provide a canon of persons and events, sacred for their original prophetic and revolutionary roles and now the object of priestly fidelity and conservatism. Such priestly concern has been modified in various ways by the wisdom of particular leaders and movements which have opened Unionists to the virtues and values of their Nationalist neighbours and their traditions.

This openness moved Protestants towards radical, indeed revolutionary, change with the small group of Presbyterians involved in the United Irishmen. More frequently the wisdom element attempted some pragmatic accommodation with its neighbours in the provisions for education in Northern Ireland, the reform programme of Terence O'Neill or climactically in the power-sharing Executive after the Sunningdale Agreement. The wisdom tradition of political Unionism is still alive and active in varying degrees among the varying parties, less evident in the Democratic Unionist Party than in the official Unionist Party with its wisdom document *The Way Forward* or among some supporters of the Alliance Party. At least that is how it appears to the outside observer. The wisdom element never simply disappears but it can become greatly obscured by the resurgent and vocal priestly tradition when the sacred values of that tradition seem threatened. So it was with the fall of Terence O'Neill and subsequently of the power-sharing Executive. The role of such fears is given proper emphasis in the report, *Breaking Down the Enmity*.

In recent times few directly prophetic voices offering transformation in fidelity have been heard within the Unionist political tradition. The prophetic stance of Corrymeela, basically Presbyterian in provenance, is not political or Unionist in this sense. I should make it clear that a prophetic voice among Unionists does not mean the substitution of a united Ireland for a United Kingdom any more than a prophetic voice among Nationalists should mean substituting United Kingdom for united Ireland. Prophetic voices on either side will transcend these priestly positions. Above all it should be emphasised that the prophetic voice is not the voice of violence. In the past no doubt prophetic political voices were frequently interpreted in terms of violent revolution. In Ireland and beyond, the priestly, conserving politics of Nationalism and Unionism, of the USA and USSR and of a host of political leaders too easily justifies and even sacralises violence. One test of the prophetic political voice for our time in Ireland will be its charting the way of non-violent political development.

Irish Nationalists have their own parallels to the Unionists in priestly, wisdom and prophetic voices. As usually happens in political history the prophetic voices of the past become centres of priestly concern in the present with some inevitable decline in inspirational quality. The voices of Wolfe Tone, Davis, Davitt, Connolly and Pearse have become too much the preserve of priestly fidelity, too little valued for their own wisdom-openness to various Irish traditions and no longer a source of inspiration for a new Nationalism. This should prophetically and unambiguously renounce all violence against fellow Irish people and be alert for a unity of Irish hearts that transcends traditional aspirations and divisions. It may not be arrogant to say that through the SDLP and the Forum for a New Ireland, Irish Nationalists have combined, in a remarkable way, priestly fidelity to the older Nationalist persons and events with a wisdom-openness to the others on this island who do not share that Nationalist tradition. It would, however, be foolish to pretend that these wisdom achievements have reached the threshold of the fresh

150

prophetic voice which will be necessary for the transformation required of all Irish people. Yet it is along this line of letting the conserving priestly and critical wisdom traditions interact that progress can be made in service to all Irish people in need of peace and justice. At the same time the way may be prepared for the always unanticipated prophetic voice and the radical change which may even now be at work, if unknown to us in our deafness and blindness.

The attempt to analyse any political situation, but particularly the British-Irish situation in terms drawn from the Jewish and Church traditions could confuse rather than clarify the issues. Because I believe that these three strands, so clearly identified (although not separated) in the history and literature of the Bible, are of universal application and profoundly illuminate so much of the human tangle, personal and social, I feel it proper to take that risk. It is important, however, for church people in this discussion and above all employing this means of analysis to reflect on how the tangle of the Churches may be illuminated by this means and how the Churches may contribute to what I have earlier called the liberation of politics.

The Irish Churches

The Churches have their own priestly, wisdom and prophetic dimensions. Some facile accounts of Church divisions would see the Roman Catholic (and Orthodox) as representing predominantly the priestly strand, the Anglicans the wisdom strand and the Reformed Churches the prophetic strand. Whatever truth this categorisation may have had in the very early years of the Reformation (and it had some for Roman Catholic and Reformed) the prophetic dimensions of much of the counter-reformation and later Catholic Church, the powerful wisdom dimension of Vatican II and the radical prophetic voices of third world Roman Catholics today make such analysis irrelevant. In similar ways the Anglican Church has always had a strong priestly tradition, something which the Reformed Churches developed quite quickly. Some of these Churches became later so dominated by the wisdom tradition that one could refer however crudely to nineteenth-century Protestantism as simply liberal Protestantism. The

151

historical fortunes of the Orthodox in Eastern Europe are less easy to follow in recent decades but within the tradition the wisdom tones of Clement of Alexandria in the third century and the prophetic voice of John Chrysostom in the fifth century have a continuing and valued history.

The Irish Churches have their own peculiarities in their presentation of the gospel of Jesus Christ, in their relationships to one another and in their relationships to social and political problems. Because the gospel cannot be presented in any pure form divorced from the historical setting of culture and politics, including inter-church relations, I will concentrate on the gospel in its Irish setting with special reference to inter-Church relations. I take it for granted here that how the Churches relate to one another in any situation today has important influence on the credibility and intelligibility of the gospel they preach. This is intensified in Ireland because of their apparent association with hostile and sometimes warring political communities. Above all if they are to invoke the insights of the biblical tradition in attempting to illuminate and offer moral guidance on political issues of justice and peace, they must honestly examine their own positions and relationships in the light of the same biblical traditions.

The priestly conserving tradition in all the Churches refers them back to the foundational events of the New Testament and various classic developments since. These foundational events and classic developments were themselves the fruit of priestly, wisdom and prophetic persons, events and insights but primarily of the person and event of Jesus Christ in the New Testament. The critical and crucial transformation occurred in Jesus. No subsequent person or event may be allowed to undermine him and his achievement. Fidelity to Jesus, his message and work of salvation is essential and so is the priestly vocation of Christians to that fidelity. Yet the very pre-eminence of Jesus beyond all others involves universality, his being available to all, salvific for all, but also his being a mirror or reflexion and concentration of all. He is the first-born of all creation (Col. 1:15) — a typical wisdom insight and an indication of how the believer's openness to the whole human condition can lead to a fuller understanding of Jesus. Teilhard de Chardin and Vatican II had a powerful awareness of how the wider human wisdom in personal, cultural and political as well as religious achievements can, however unwittingly, explore and express aspects of Jesus which can enrich through dialogue Christians and their faith. A truly priestly fidelity to Jesus will be alert to the dialogue with all, of which Paul VI spoke so effectively in his encyclical *Ecclesiam Suam* and which characterised so much of Vatican II. In all its limitations, so obvious in hindsight, the intellectual and cultural dialogue of nineteenth-century Protestant theologians and Church leaders extended the understanding by Christians of their own tradition beyond the self-enclosure of a fundamentalist and fundamentally unchristian priestly conservatism.

Fidelity to the unique historical events of Jesus Christ and openness to the universal human expressions of creation and incarnation do not exhaust the continuing explosive potential of Christian faith. Whether viewed as historical past or universal present the person and achievements of Jesus are still critically future, until he comes again, when the Kingdom shall finally break through. The pressure of the future, of the transformation that lies ahead must, as Jesus frequently warned his disciples, keep the Churches awake, alert to the prophetic voices and transforming possibilities which may come upon them at any time. When the priestly ascetic figure of Pius XII yielded in 1958 to the open, wise, fatherly figure of John XXIII, he issued his gentle but prophetic call to Council. As the expressed wisdom of the Council fathers at Vatican II encountered a more critical situation in Latin America, a prophetic way emerged from the Latin American Bishops' Conference at Medellín in 1968 which has provided a fresh impetus for transformation within the Catholic Church. Similar stories can be told of other Churches. The World Council of Churches, which grew out of the ecumenical wisdom dialogue of the different priestly traditions in the earlier part of the century, reached a radical prophetic stance similar to that of the Latin American Church in the later 1960s. All this applies in various ways within the Irish context to the Irish Churches. Their own ecumenical wisdom dialogue, for all its frustrations, limitations and fragility, has endorsed priestly fidelity while attempting to liberate it from biblical or doctrinal fundamentalism. Fundamentalism has disfigured the various Churches in various ways from the beginning. The disputes of Jesus and the Pharisees over the sabbath and the Judaising controversies involving Peter and Paul were re-echoed in later Church disputes between priestly, wisdom and prophetic tendencies.

These were seldom resolved without pain and patience and sometimes had to remain unresolved. How radical and transformative developments in Christian life and belief have liberated the Churches at many points in history is sometimes obscured because the prophetic voice of one council or move-ment is inevitably and properly projected as the conserving priestly voice later. A new prophetic challenge is then called for.

At least the Irish Churches should be sensitive to this history as they confront their own needs. Priestly fidelity is not in short supply among Irish Church-people although it may too easily become priestly fundamentalism. Church leaders, theologians and the believing communities must maintain their fidelity but distinguish it from fundamentalism. Doctrinal fundamentalism in Ireland is compounded by political fundamentalism. Anti-papal fundamentalism has clearly a strong political dimension. But how far does political resentment derived from history, make Catholics and Pro-testants appear grudging in discussing, for example, shared sacraments and mixed marriages? Is there no fundamentalism of a partly political kind at work in our conflicting Christian fidelities?

The wisdom practice of theologians can provide a useful critique of our fidelity. Protestant sense of Bible has helped Catholics already as Catholic sense of sacrament has had its impact on Protestants. But deeper, more searching dialogue through mutual criticism and mutual acceptance has a long way to go before we are ready for prophetic voices and move-ments of inter-Church unity. The present concern is not some radical transformation of the Irish Churches into the one great Church but a more profound conversion to one another that will release them from their quasi-political Babylonian captivity.

Such releasing of one another from the priestly political traditions of Nationalism and Unionism will occur through heightened ecumenical programmes of shared prayer, study and service to the deprived, particularly the deprived of the

154

other tradition. Along these lines the growth of their mutual conversion and shared liberation will at the same time and, perhaps, the same pace, liberate politics and politicians from their priestly fundamentalism without their having to betray their proper politics.

The discerning of the three different strands in any political or religious tradition may help fidelity to avoid fundamentalism, dialogue to develop without abandonment of roots and prophecy to emerge as pointing the way to creative transformation. In that process the Churches themselves must seek, through their own priestly, wisdom and prophetic strands, to fulfil their obligation to let the gospel liberate politics and to let politicians get on with their urgent and difficult tasks.

The Anglo-Irish Agreement attempts to do justice to the priestly traditions of Nationalism and Unionism in an open 'Wisdom' way which could have radical new creation possibilities. The present Unionists' priestly resistance must be addressed in a sensitive manner which will encourage their own wisdom traditions and people without driving more Nationalists back into being dominated by their conservative, priestly positions. For politicians and Church leaders there is a new call to enable the new creation prevail over the old chaos. The possibilities exist but they are very fragile.

12.

The Christian
in Politics

THE CESSATION of religion as a politically significant factor in human society has been proclaimed more than once in the last two hundred years by both its supporters and its opponents. Voltaire's call *'Ecrasez l'infame'*, referring immediately to the Catholic Church but with wider implications, influenced successive, successful and unsuccessful, revolutionary movements in Europe. In North America and the Anglo-Saxon world generally a more benign separation of Church and State seemed, by the time of the election of John Kennedy, President of the United States in 1960, to have effectively, if sympathetically, separated religion and politics. Meanwhile the whole of Eastern Europe, under the hegemony of the USSR, had set out on a path to eliminate religion from society as regressive and subversive. The rest of the world seemed set to follow the American and European example of politics without religion, if that example had not already been anticipated. The 1980s reveal quite a different world from the 1960s. Close interaction between religion and politics has emerged all over the world. Movements, people and places like Solidarity, Khomeini, Amritsar, Moral Majority, Beirut, Liberation Theology, Paisley and once again Jerusalem, have revealed the depth and the intensity of the connections between the religious and political aspirations of human beings. This applies to the so-called advanced countries like the United States (and increasingly the United Kingdom) as well as the newly emergent countries like Iran and India, to countries officially hostile to religion in Eastern Europe and to countries officially indifferent to it in the

West. For all the twentieth century's advance in science and technology, with the accompanying phenomena of urbanisation and secularisation, the contemporary secular city is unable to escape its religious *döppelganger*. The politics of the most secular city must still come to terms with those ultimate human needs and aspirations which the great religions have discerned, expressed and organised.

Many politicians are themselves of course authentic religious believers. Such great architects of modern Europe as Charles de Gaulle and Konrad Adenauer, Robert Schumann and Alcide de Gasperi were openly committed to Christian religious belief and practice. So was the great architect of modern Ireland, Eamon de Valera. Active politicians in Western countries tend to bracket their religious beliefs in dealing with their usually pluralist electorate. And few of them have reflected in print on the significance of those beliefs. Dag Hammarskjold was a very unusual phenomenon in his struggle to combine, admittedly in the (ambiguous) privacy of a diary, his concern, as a public and political servant, with the development of his Christian faith. Garret FitzGerald may be even more unusual in combining an interest in theology with his political involvement as Taoiseach. His regular theological reading and his attendance at theological seminars and lectures are well known. This interest has inevitably issued in some published reflexions on the relation between Christianity and politics. Some early indications of this appears in his *Towards a New Ireland* (1972). More developed ideas were presented to the Annual Conference of the Irish Theological Association in January 1977 and published reflexions suggest the need for the reconsideration *Theology: An Irish Dialogue* (ed. D. Lane). A further article appeared in *The Furrow* under the title 'The Politician as a Christian' (1978).

Garret FitzGerald has not attempted to develop a systematic view of the Christian in politics, still less a Christian theology of politics. However, this interest in theology, his own political preoccupations, domestic and foreign, and his published reflections suggest the need for the reconsideration of the Christian in politics in the context of current theological thinking and of contemporary politics.

157

As in so many profoundly human issues the more interesting questions are the oldest. The early Christians were confronted by their pagan fellow-citizens of the Roman Empire with the question of how far they could be true citizens of the Empire. The Apologists of the second century were trying to establish their *bona fides* as citizens, as people who were loyal and indeed of value to the Empire. The intermittent severe persecution to which they were subjected by the imperial authorities into the fourth century, until their final acceptance by the Emperor Constantine, showed how difficult it was for them to establish that they were, in a phrase from later times, politically reliable. In the suspicion of their political seriousness and reliability these early Christians were not unique. Their Jewish forebears had had at times to endure similar treatment. And both Jewish and Christian posterity, together with adherents of other major and minor religions, have found themselves under threat because of their allegiance to a world and a power beyond the immediately historical and political.

The relativisation of human history by eschatology, the final destiny of humanity beyond history, involves inevitably a relativisation of politics. The Christian view of this world as passing, and quickly according to many of the first Christians such as Paul, could be and was taken to mean that the affairs of this world, including public or political affairs, were unimportant. It would be impossible to deny that such an attitude to worldly affairs played an important role in Christian belief and practice over the centuries and that it is still around. In the contemporary debate the criticism of Marx and Engels has become classic. According to them the alienation which religion expresses and reinforces prevents true political and economic change. Religion keeps the oppressed resigned as they wait for the world to come and is exploited by the oppressors for their own purposes. 'The abolition of religion as the illusory happiness of the people is required for their real happiness.' As 'the opium of the people', 'the fantastic realisation of the human essence', it must be removed to make way for the true realisation (K. Marx and F. Engels, *On Religion*, Moscow 1955).

E. P. Thompson, in his magisterial *The Making of the English Working Class* (1963), sharply criticises the role of early Methodism in keeping the poor industrial workers in in their place. In the Irish situation a series of critics, before and after Jim Larkin, have seen the Catholic Church as endorsing political and economic structures by appeal to the reward awaiting the poor in heaven. The current spread of Church involvement in liberation movements around the world has met with sharp questions by supporters and opponents of these movements. How far can Christians (above all priests and Church leaders) be committed to historical, political liberation, given their commitment to a spiritual world beyond history as the true destiny of humanity (cf. Camillo Torres, *Revolutionary Priest*, 1971)?

The enterprise of liberation theology, Latin American in origin, is aimed at providing a positive answer to this question. It has of course its own political and theological critics. The theological critics see it as surrendering the transcendent and eschatological (beyond-this-world and beyond-history) dimensions of Christianity, the very features which created the difficulty in the first place. The political critics, ecclesiastical and secular, reject what they see as its endorsement of socialism (for some, Marxism) as the key to political analysis and transformation. This reverses the socialist criticism of Christianity and the Churches as endorsing the capitalist *status quo* in the name of keeping free of politics and concentrating on spiritual and heavenly salvation.

All this could seem very remote from the island of Ireland where Christians, Catholic and Protestant, lay and clerical take Christian political involvement for granted. For some of them the primary issues are constitutional: United Kingdom or United Ireland; lawful and unlawful, violent and nonviolent means to that objective. For others, matters of family life engage them explicitly as Christians. Although discussions of economics do not generally involve any invocation of Christian terms, social justice including economic justice at home and in relation to the third world attracts such explicit Christian interest. Most political issues in Ireland, like most politically aware people, have some Christian connection.

This may seem an overwhelming response to the charge that Christians cannot take politics seriously. If anything

Irish Christians, as particular kinds of Christians, seem to take their politics too seriously. Getting the Christian Churches out of politics in Ireland seem to many a more appropriate move than asking Christians to take politics seriously. Official Church involvement is seen as divisive and destructive by many Irish and Christian citizens and politicians in the areas of constitutional politics and of family law. Such Christians can and should help liberate politics from destructive involvement with their Churches and at the same time liberate their Churches from the self-destructive aspects of that involvement. Their attempts to help will have ecclesial and political implications.

At the ecclesial or Church level, concerned Christians will be seeking to promote inter-Church relations. The closer the Irish Churches come together as believing and worshipping communities in shared Christian faith, hope and love, the more liberated they become from their traditionally divisive, ethnic, cultural and political affiliations. This will allow more freedom to Church leaders or clergy to concentrate on their pastoral roles and to do that jointly in ways that will render their Christian witness more credible. The Christian call to repentance, forgiveness and reconciliation, which applies to the Churches in their (frequently hostile) divisions, must be answered by all Christians; and by Irish Christians for that further reason of promoting civic and political peace. Christian citizens in Ireland have as part of both their religious and political tasks, the duty of promoting ecumenical growth among the Churches.

This should not be taken to suggest that Irish Church leaders are negligent in promoting reconciliation at different levels. It is more a matter of emphasising the roles of individual Christian citizens and politicians in supporting the ecumenical efforts of their Churches and so freeing them from the limitations of older political connections. This will also be furthered by Christian citizens and politicians engaging in political reconciliation, developing the attitudes, the contacts and structures in which political movement is possible. Those engaged in such movement and the accompanying structures will have to recognise and respect the different traditions and protect the historic, often fearful and alienated minorities which have emerged North and South. This seems to be a central goal of the recent Hillsborough agreement, however successful it may be in persuading Northern unionists of that. Related to that respect for divergent religious and political traditions is the call to respect divergent moral traditions. Such recognition is particularly sensitive in family issues within the Irish context. To address that difficulty it will be useful to raise another basic question which may be addressed to Christians, and particularly Catholic Christians, in politics.

Can Christians in Politics be Free and Democratic?

Without attempting a historical overview it may be said that the different Christian Churches, Catholic, Orthodox and Reformed have been associated in practice with very authoritarian political regimes and activities and that this has operated after the advent of democratic forms and structures, to the frustration and sometimes the undermining of democracy. In such historical examples many practical and justifying causes may be advanced, such as threats of chaos or communism. More principled criticism of the Churches' endorsement or at least acceptance of authoritarianism in government may be found in some of their own doctrinal and theological traditions such as Roman Catholicism's own strongly developed view of central Church authority which may appear to endorse a strong central state authority. Anglicanism's recognition of the head of state as head of the Church or the Reformed vision of the theocratic state or the Lutheran doctrine of the two Kingdoms may make the political authority immune to Christian criticism. Orthodoxy's successive versions of Caesaro-papism suggested similar immunity for the political authority. Yet the early and critical relativisation of imperial authority by the one Christian Church, and the recovery of that in recent centuries, combined with a renewed sense of the dignity of the human person and its consequences in human rights language, provide some effectual intellectual Christian backing for major aspects of democratic theory. These include limitations on political authority, respect for individual human rights and participation by people in their own governance. How these democratic aims are realised in practice may vary quite considerably and they are open to interpretations which may seem exploitative and indeed anti-democratic to various minorities and even majorities in a particular country.

In the particular country of Ireland the various Churches are open to charges of anti-democratic exploitation. The period up to disestablishment in 1869 saw the Church of Ireland very much in such a position. One might accuse the Presbyterian Church and other Protestant bodies in Northern Ireland of such practices in the situation leading up to and resulting from the partition of Ireland in 1920. And of course similar accusations are made against the Catholic Church in the Republic since its inception as an independent state in 1921. There is little point in trying to discuss and adjudicate these charges here in all their tangled history, emotional power and frequently exaggerated expression. It would be more useful to try to examine how principle and practice might operate in future if Irish Christians are to be taken seriously as genuinely democratic and free in their politics.

The issue of freedom is central, the freedom of citizens and politicians to seek the good of all citizens, irrespective of creed or sex or class. Limitations on that freedom may be of different kinds and origins. Shortage of resources, particularly economic resources, is a common limitation today as politicians defend themselves for failing to achieve some aspect of the common good, such as equal pay for women. Historic identity may be another, as Nationalist or Unionist politicians in Ireland maintain that their supporters cannot accept such a development as the Hillsborough agreement. Class interest is undoubtedly a very serious and insidious limitation on political freedom in Ireland as privileged and powerful groups in business, the professions and trade unions, distort and inhibit the promotion of the overall good of the community. Religious interests may operate in a similarly inhibiting way and sometimes reinforce other limiting forces of national identity or class interest.

The role of the Orange Order and the more explicit expression of 'Protestant Politics' in Northern Ireland appear to reflect one side of the directly religious limitation on the freedom of politicians to seek the good of the whole community. The directives of the Catholic hierarchy, particularly on aspects of family life and education, appear to reflect

162

the other. Debates about the reality behind these appearances are always intense and acrimonious. At least it may be said that both sides have a case to answer. The forms of Catholic influence turn on the relation between the teaching authority of the bishops and the decision-making authority on political issues of citizens and politicians. Bishops maintain, most recently and emphatically in Ireland in their oral submissions to the Forum for a New Ireland, that they claim and seek no political authority and fully accept the separation of Church and State. They do, however, claim to speak authoritatively on moral issues, including social and political moral issues such as social justice, war and other political violence, as well as social issues affecting family and sexual morality. It would obviously be unreal to claim to be moral teachers and ignore the great social moral issues of the day. But does this not constrain Catholic citizens and politicians in their seeking the good of all? Are their consciences not already bound by their commitment as Catholics to follow the bishops' directives and ignore the claims of other groups in society? To be free in their own political decisions must they not leave their Catholicism aside?

Full answers to these questions would be long and complicated. Yet a number of important points should be made briefly and clearly. Church authorities claim to teach morality, not to prescribe or proscribe state laws, the domain of the politicians. Catholic Church authorities speak to Catholics; legislators deal with all the citizens. The morality, which the Catholic Church teaches, addresses social as well as personal issues. In this the Church seeks to promote the good of society by clarifying the moral issues, exhorting and motivating its members, and providing support for the living out of this teaching from its own resources of community, word and sacrament. This fulfilment of its social role by the Church is described in Gospel terms as preaching and promoting the Kingdom of God announced and inaugurated by Jesus. State law and other state activity are not part of the resources of the Church as it seeks to fulfil its task in society.

Politics and politicians can benefit from this work of the Church in society. As members of the Church they may be directly engaged in it themselves. Yet their task of seeking the common good and respecting the freedom of all citizens

163

by state-law and administration is utterly distinct and clearly separate from that of the Church. The common good must be both good and common, that is morally approvable in a way recognisable by the community. This can lead to difficulties because of the intractability of certain problems and the diversity of the community. In difficult situations, of violence or the abuse of drugs or drink, very restrictive measures reducing the normal freedom of citizens and so affecting the common good, may be necessary and justified as the lesser of evils. In others diversity is so great that some group may find its claims diminished for the sake of social cohesion or some greater good of the community as a whole. How to combine the overall good of the community with personal freedoms and other claims, demands great commitment and skill from the politicians. The skill, commitment and responsibility belong properly to the politician and legislator, not to the Church leader. He may and sometimes should offer suggestions and criticism based on his concern for the moral well-being of society but without claiming any special political responsibility and insight. In this he is at one with other citizens and not apart from or above them. Further qualifications and distinctions might be made in all this but as in all areas of human behaviour much will depend on the sensitive awareness of particular agents. Bishops and other Church leaders must be especially sensitive to the danger of manipulating, however unconsciously, citizens or politicians in areas where political judgments do not coincide with their own. The freedom of Catholic politicians to discharge their political tasks is essential to the health of democracy in Ireland and elsewhere. For that reason alone it is also essential to the health of the Catholic Church. By fully respecting this freedom Catholic Church leaders will be discharging an important part of their role of promoting the Kingdom in society and, in the Irish context, offering a lead to other religious and group interests that may seek to distort the democratic process to their own benefit. Commitment to politics and freedom in politics should be accepted marks of Christians and Catholics today and not the source of question marks.

13.

Artisans of a New Creation: Peadar O'Donnell and J. G. McGarry

CHRISTIAN faith is faith in God become human, in human beings as images and children of God, participants in the divine activities of creation and new creation. Christian faith reflexion or theology emerges in the story of that central human being, Jesus Christ, but also in the stories of all human beings. Two such stories of Irish people are briefly considered here in what might be considered primary exercises in narrative theology. In the context of this book I see J. G. McGarry and Peadar O'Donnell as struggling to overcome chaos, destruction and desert in different dimensions of Irish society. Modest people themselves, they combined a genuine creativity in thought and action with a flinty determination in pursuit of their purposes. O'Donnell might well be described as an artist for his literary work and McGarry had very developed artistic and cultural interests. Yet with their country origins and ways they would have felt more comfortable with the description artisan. So it is as artisans of a new creation in Ireland at this period that they become subjects of theological analysis here.

PEADAR O'DONNELL – CHALLENGE TO IRISH CHRISTIANS

The astonishing range of gifts, activities and achievements of Peadar O'Donnell over such a blessed length of days will provide his biographers with exciting and demanding challenges. The republican armed rebel, the land agitator, the organiser of the potato-pickers in Scotland, the school-teacher, the editor, the novelist, the socialist, the civil libertarian, the international farm organiser, the anti-war activist . . . the list could go on. And it is clearly not the list of somebody who moved through a series of short-term, fashionable causes. The engagement with each was deep and persistent, issuing in suffering, privation and even prison at times.

I knew Peadar O'Donnell over many years. I have admired and been disturbed by him for much longer. The admiration and disturbance go back to my student days at Maynooth in the early fifties and my reading of *The Bell*. I have therefore felt over a long time that he was challenging Christians in Ireland to take their Christianity more seriously and in ways and on issues which they might easily avoid. Given the richness of the life these challenging ways and issues seem countless. I must drastically select therefore and try to capture his challenge to Christianity under a few crude headings.

The Outsider

To adopt as primary characteristic of Peadar O'Donnell 'the outsider', must seem paradoxical now so many of the established names in Irish life honour him. For all his activities and achievements, for all the honour now paid, he has remained outside the power-structure of Irish life. This was how he began his life in poverty in Donegal and how he completed his life in peace in Dublin.

To be born in Ireland at the end of the last century was to face the fate of the outsider, the peripheral, the fringe person. To be born in Donegal (or Mayo, my own home county) made one doubly peripheral in an Empire that raced red over so much of the globe. Geography and politics combined to render the peoples of the fringe invisible to the centre. Replacing London by Dublin, Empire by Republic has reduced but not entirely removed the mental distance separating centre and periphery, insider and outsider. Of course Finglas can be as distant as Fanad for myopic and established insiders. Peadar O'Donnell's early engagement with the peripheral tatie-hokers or peasant farmers of the West was quickly supplemented by his concern for the deprived of Glasgow, Belfast and Dublin. His outsider status was born of the politics and geography of Donegal but it was very soon deepened by his identification with the cause of poverty-stricken city-dwellers, exploited both as employed and as unemployed. Because the powers of politics and commerce (the powers of this world) exploited or neglected these poor, O'Donnell could never be part of them. Only in the transformed society of his republican, democratic and above all socialist dreams, in which there were no outsiders, might he have been able to adjust and accommodate rather than agitate.

How far we are from such a society in Ireland today scarcely requires comment. Peadar O'Donnell's recent pamphlet *Not Yet, Emmet* might in another idiom have borne the title *Outsider Yet, O'Donnell.*

O'Donnell was not of course the only outsider of his time whose status and role turned on his practical engagement with the excluded in our society. As in all revolutionary situations fringe-people came to the centre. Of these Eamon de Valera was undoubtedly the most famous, the most enduring and by some standards and for some people the most successful. His move to the centre of Irish politics with the foundation of Fianna Fáil and his subsequent election to government contrasts neatly with O'Donnell's continuing peripheral status. Despite his fringe origins and the persistent faithfulness of the fringe-people of Donegal, Mayo and Kerry, de Valera did not manage to restructure Irish political life sufficiently to overcome the vast difference between the centre and the fringe, between the established and the disestablished. A move to the centre without profound social analysis and commitment may change some of the personnel at the centre. It cannot transform the centre-periphery relationship. Of this O'Donnell had always been conscious and for this he had always remained an outsider.

There were Church people in these years who had something of O'Donnell's status and sense of the outsider. Unfortunately they were usually unable to develop that sense in any systematic way and were often afraid of the socialist implications of their own deepest instincts. A thoroughly conservative bishop like Bishop Lucey of Cork had a feeling for the marginalisation of the people of West Cork and for the blindness and apathy at the centre in their regard. His fears of communism as well as a restricted vision of Christianity may have been responsible for his inability to encourage

167

radical thinkers and activists like O'Donnell in their search for a more just society. Fellow Donegal-man Fr James McDyer did not have the same difficulties about the needs and possibilities of socialist reform, although his admirable enterprise did not reap the reward it might have. On a grander scale Canon John Hayes of Muintir na Tire attempted to revitalise Irish rural life but without any penetrating social and economic analysis. More closely associated in mind and action with Peadar O'Donnell was Fr John Fahey of the diocese of Clonfert. These Church-people in varying degrees were outsiders, outside the dominant social, economic and political power-structures and concerned for the neglected and excluded, particularly in rural Ireland. They had their counterparts in urban Ireland also. Yet there was a marked and at times a hostile distance between the social and economic attitudes and activities of people like O'Donnell and those of the socially concerned clergy. Outsiderdom had varying degrees and O'Donnell was many degrees beyond clerical outsiders. The option for the poor and certainly the social analysis and shared suffering which have accompanied it in Latin America over the last twenty years were not really characteristic of Irish clergy over the last eighty years. Recent developments among Irish missionaries like Fr Niall O'Brien in the third world have had inevitable repercussions among some home-based priests, brothers, sisters and lay-folk and may lead to the adoption of ideas and practices by Irish Christians for which O'Donnell had to suffer at the hands of earlier Church leaders.

The 'outsider' phenomenon, which O'Donnell exemplifies to Ireland in this century, has more human and Christian significance than simply being ahead of one's time, opposed to the exploiters, and critical of the establishment. Christians in particular do well to reflect on the 'outsider' in their own traditions. That trenchant prophetic social critic of the eighth century before Christ, Amos, is a representative figure as prophetic outsider calling the religious and political establishment to order. He dismisses sacrifices and solemn prayer assemblies as repulsive to God because of the exploitation of the widow, the orphan and the stranger. Other Hebrew prophets were called to this outsider role of critic of power in place and place-men in power. For Christians the climax was reached with Jesus Christ, a nobody (mere carpenter, son of Mary and Joseph) and from nowhere (can anything good come out of Nazareth?). Identifying himself with the outcasts and sinners in society, eating and drinking with prostitutes and tax-collectors, feeding the hungry and healing the sick, he preached an upside-down Kingdom in which the mighty would be put down from their thrones, the last first and the first last, the lame walk, the blind see, the prisoners set free and the poor have the good news preached to them. Final test for entry to this Kingdom would be, after his example, feeding the hungry, visiting the prisoners, and caring for the least ones, the marginalised (Mt. 25). It was not a manifesto and a life-style the establishment could accept without ceasing to be an establishment. And so Jesus was condemned as an agitator and executed outside the city — the definitive outsider. His God, the God of outsiders and marginalised, triumphed over the final exclusion of a criminal death by raising him from the dead.

When the powers in place, at centre, had done their worst by killing him, they were confronted with their own final failure. The crucified one was to manifest the destiny of all the excluded and marginalised in resurrection which they were called to share even then and now. The upside-down Kingdom is among us. Even now the outcasts are to enjoy the table-fellowship with the risen Lord and with one another. The last, neglected and marginalised are to be given priority. This is the constant challenge facing Christians which they so frequently ignore as they surrender to their insider privileges and comforts. One of the providential ways of reminding Christians of their call is the emergence of prophetic outsiders, sharing something of the vocation and privation of Amos, of Jeremiah and of Jesus himself. It may not be too much to claim that for Irish Christians with eyes to see, Peadar O'Donnell played something of that role of prophetic 'outsider'.

Anti-Imperialist

Peadar O'Donnell, 'anti-imperialist', must sound dated after Empire. More positive political terms such as republican and socialist and civil libertarian convey more immediately something of the content of his developing political positions. Later I shall discuss such content and concerns. Yet there is in 'anti-imperialism' a continuing clue to his thought and work which takes further his role as 'outsider' and suggests continuing challenge to Irish Christians.

The end of Empire does not mean the end of imperialism. No particular Empire, not even the British Empire, of such immediate concern to O'Donnell in his youth, exhausts the possibilities or actualities of imperialism even in its own time or within its own boundaries. Imperialism may have as many political faces and phases as it has economic, cultural and religious aspects. To stand with the marginalised is to stand against imperialism, sometimes no more than 'gombeen' imperialism, but nonetheless the assertion of superiority and control over the freedoms and destinies of sister-and-brother human beings. O'Donnell's support for the workers in Scotland, his land agitation as well as his more conventional struggles for republicanism, socialism and civil liberties, all reflect this opposition to the imperial mind and structure that so often affect even self-conscious republicans (USA style) and self-conscious socialists (USSR style). At his best he rose above the imperialist intentions and activities of even some Irish republicans, socialists and civil libertarians by his persistent commitment to the poor and fringe and by his continuing analysis of the structures of constraint and exploitation. Civil liberties were as much his cause as socialism or republicanism, as his editorship of *The Bell*, for example, showed and during years when many of his more famous contemporaries could at best manage one out of these three: republicanism, socialism or civil liberties.

It was on the basis of anti-imperialism, particularly in its socialist mode, that his hopes for Irish unity were founded. His generous vision of his fellow-countrymen, who were Northern, Protestant and working-class, inspired his belief in a coming together of the excluded and marginalised in a single socialist republic on this island. Perhaps he was too much in advance of his time for those republican and Catholic on the one hand, and for those Unionist and Protestant on the other, to both of whom anti-imperialism meant simply anti-British. On this basis they adopted directly conflicting stances — against or for Britain, rather than against or for imperialism.

Could it be that the Unionists and loyalists were and are resisting a form of Irish imperialism as Nationalists and republicans have resisted forms of British imperialism? Does the basically anti-imperialist stance of O'Donnell lead to equal criticism of republican assertions of superiority and control over Unionists' destiny? Must articles 2 and 3 of the 1937 Constitution have something of that ring for Unionists? Can they be deleted without apparent surrender to British Unionist forms of imperialism? Must Ireland continue to endure the clash of two imperialisms in bombs and bullets and blood? Or can these 'imperialised', if I may use the expression, make common cause against all imperialists, British, Ulster, Irish? Is it possible to speak of a republic anyway with so much residual imperialism, political, economic, cultural and religious still around?

In recent years Peadar O'Donnell's engagement with issues of world-peace has exposed another facet of his anti-imperialism. War and the culture of war are typically imperialist. And it may be that we can only break out of the viciously circular conflict of imperialisms, as between the USA and the USSR as well as in Northern Ireland, by recognising the imperial nature of war and developing effective unarmed anti-imperial strategies. The Ireland-India nexus in the breaking of Empire might be taken a step further if Irish people were to integrate the thought and strategy of Gandhi into their quarrels at home and their service of peace-keeping abroad. The anti-imperialism of O'Donnell which produced the armed rebel in his youth might well find its completion in some Gandhi-like form today.

The theme of anti-imperialism, its rethinking beyond anti-British and its transformation into unarmed strategy for radical social and economic as well as political change, certainly presents challenges to Irish people. Does it concern in particular Irish Christians? What has been discussed under anti-imperialism in terms of justice and freedom and self-government belongs to a social order which Christians rightly approve of and of whose absence they ought to disapprove. Social thinking among Christians over the last hundred years has reached, laboriously and slowly, many of these conclusions about a just society. The laboriousness and slowness meant that Peadar O'Donnell among others had to suffer for

171

his greater speed and more active commitment. Most Irish Christians in practice and in theory are still some distance from the validly moral and basically Christian conclusions which he reached quite some time ago. So he remains a challenge.

Anti-imperialism has, however, deeper resonances for Christians, if they have ears to hear. The Kingdom, the upside-down Kingdom, which Jesus proclaimed and inaugurated, for which he died and which broke through in his resurrection, embodies, properly understood, the end of imperialism. The exaltation of the humble which Mary, according to Luke's gospel, hymned in the 'Magnificat' prayer, does not mean that they shall inhabit the thrones from which the mighty have been put down, to lord it over the deposed in turn. The Christian revolution is not simply a turn of wheel with the people at the bottom taking over from the top people who move to bottom. In the Jesus vision of redeemed humanity there is no top or bottom, centre or periphery. 'Neither in this place nor Jerusalem shall people worship God.' Not lording it over them as the Gentiles, the imperialists do, but servants of all. The radical equality of all, called and enabled to be daughters and sons of God in and through Jesus, allows no room for superiority of race or caste or class or sex or colour. All the imperialisms the world has known and still knows in such destructive form are irreconcilable with the message and achievement of Jesus. If only Christian racists and sexists, all manner of Christian imperialists in Ireland and elsewhere, had recognised their own self-contradiction! The Irish could certainly have learned some of it from Peadar O'Donnell.

Word and Vision

Two of the dominant avocations among Irish men over two centuries have been politician and writer. Not many apart from Peadar O'Donnell have managed to combine political activity and creative writing. What may finally make him unique is his combining activist and novelist with his editor-ship of *The Bell* and his exercise of the role of social and literary critic. The debt which cultural life and critical thought in twentieth-century Ireland owes to *The Bell* and men like

172

O'Donnell and O'Faoláin is undoubtedly immense. I recall reading it avidly as a student and even attempting to promote it and its associates in an article I wrote for a student magazine in Maynooth about 1953. I was concerned with the challenge to Irish Christians and the possibilities for growth which the critical and creative talents of *The Bell* group offered to all of us in what was, it seemed, a drab and closed time in Irish intellectual and cultural life.

In presenting a more open and creative side O'Donnell as editor was resuming work he had done earlier in some of his novels and in his editorship of *An Poblacht*. One of these novels, *The Big Windows*, where the island girl marries into the glen and persuades her husband to put big windows into the house so that she may enjoy the light as she did on the island, is a parable of O'Donnell's own work in *The Bell* and elsewhere. The outsider was confronting the suspicious glen people of Ireland as a whole and offering fresh light and openness. The power of the story in its own right remains and it makes an interesting contrast with that perhaps more famous 'glen' novel of O'Donnell's contemporary, *The Valley of the Squinting Windows* by Brinsley MacNamara. With O'Donnell creative vision always dominated over the suspicious squint.

Vision and its expression in word were an urgent requirement of Irish society and the Irish Church at this time. I like to think that the challenge of *The Bell* to Irish Christians was to some extent taken up by the founding of *The Furrow* in 1950. Founder-editor J. G. (Gerry) McGarry was, like O'Donnell, a countryman from the western seaboard. Despite his position at Maynooth he remained there and in the Irish Catholic Church as a whole an outsider, on the fringe. But he had a vision and he formed for Irish Christians a link between the Big Windows of O'Donnell and his critical and creative contemporaries and the Church whose windows Pope John XXIII finally threw open with the summoning of the Second Vatican Council. It was then that *The Furrow* really began to thrive and McGarry as its editor to flourish. There had been the lean, hard years of the fifties and there were misunderstandings and rejections to come. Yet McGarry like O'Donnell attained something of the celebrity status of recognised and effective outsider. Interiorly McGarry remained fresh and alert and became increasingly serene until he died rather prematurely in a car accident in 1977. A close contemporary of O'Donnell, he paralleled his work at *The Bell* in his own effective editorial activities. An outsider to the end, away from the corridors of ecclesiastical power and its temptations to imperialism, McGarry presented his own challenge to Church people, but also to politicians, writers and *The Bell*. The human creativity which *The Bell* encouraged at an uncreative time in Irish life should have reminded Christians of the creative Spirit of God which issues in such diverse forms of new life. The creative word in particular has rich Jewish and Christian associations. To presume to worship that God of creation while ignoring human creativity in literature and the arts, for example, merits once again the scathing critique of an Amos. *The Bell* was also willing to offer it. Scarcer even than Irish creative writing at the time was coherent critical comment. And naturally criticism was even less acceptable. But without the free play of criticism the truth which in Christian terms is to set humanity free is obscured and evaded. The call to move beyond obscurity and evasion, which so easily affect everybody's life, is to a truly human but also deeply Christian task, as Jesus and his prophetic predecessors fully understood and sharply exposed. In all this activity O'Donnell as novelist, editor and critic challenged Church and Christian. Through McGarry and *The Furrow* that world of politics and culture began to receive something of a Christian challenge in return. But that takes us to a closer look at our second artisan.

J. G. McGARRY, EDITOR OF THE FURROW 1950-77

In many ways the Irish and the Churches in Ireland devote too much time and energy to self-examination. The search for identity can become a neurotic dissipation of whatever identity one has, and another kind of hazard occurs by reaching for reassurance through a superficial recital of strengths and achievements in face of real or imagined difficulties. Any attempt to assess the impact of the late J. G. McGarry and in particular of his work as Editor of *The Furrow* is exposed to these very dangers as it cannot be divorced from the context of Irish Church and society 1950-77.

174

In many ways the most distinctive contribution of *The Furrow* and its late Editor to Irish Church life was the change of style in communication within the Church which they promoted and reflected. A trivial illustration of this was his dropping of the reverential preamble (plain or coloured) to the names of contributors on the cover at the beginning of the second year of publication. This recalls one of his own favourite stories about the previous priorities of Irish journalism in Church affairs. During the promotion of the national collection for Maynooth in the late forties he had occasion to visit the offices of the Dublin daily papers. On his way out one of the staff related the feeling of near panic of some staff on discovering that the presses were almost rolling, with the '+' before the name of a deceased bishop omitted in his death notice. The McGarry chuckle revealed his own sense of proportion in these matters.

One of his favourite quotations to students about the style being the man could be readily adapted to a more general principle of the style of communication making the community. Whether he explicitly adverted to this formulation or not, his practice over twenty-seven years expressed the principle and enormously influenced and was in turn influenced by changes in the Irish Church and Irish society.

It is important to understand his implicit grasp of the more general principle that the style of communicating makes or at least shapes, the community. McGarry was no effete style-for-style's-sake man. Neither did he favour certain 'journalistic' practices of sensationalising, exaggerating or simplifying in order to catch attention even in the interests of otherwise neglected truth. He paid a certain amount of attention to packaging as it is called and emphasised the need to produce an attractive-looking, well-written and readable journal. These were necessary but not at all sufficient conditions for the communication he espoused.

Central to that communication was respect for persons. *The Furrow* did not deal in point-scoring, still less in personal abuse. McGarry himself seemed incapable of either. He retained his countryman's innocence of and disinterest in the personal and political infighting of his academic or

175

clerical colleagues. This occasionally led him into errors of judgment but innocence is not naïveté and he often showed surprising country shrewdness in assessing people and situations. His respect for the person did exclude much of the gossip which is as characteristic of clerical life as of any other. But he was not unfairly critical in private, he was not fawning in public. His other-respect and his self-respect were two sides of the same coin. The public face reflected in *The Furrow* was, so far as these features were concerned, identical with the private face revealed at the dining-table or in the study. Essential to respect for persons is coherence between face-to-face and behind-the-back attitudes and expressions; a coherence that is not automatically attributable to clergy or laity in the Church. McGarry had it to an unusual degree.

Such coherence gave a strength and confidence to his editorial work that seemed to develop with the years. Because his attention was focused not on personalities but on issues, *The Furrow* gradually acquired the skill and the confidence to handle the most sensitive issues in an objective and enriching manner. The debate between Denis O'Callaghan and various contributors on the admittedly tired subject of *Humane Vitae* was a good example of this. So were the couple of articles on the succession to Armagh, in 1977, various articles on Celibacy reaching back into the 1960s, the reports on Vatican II mainly by Sean O'Riordan, the survey of review material on marriage and divorce by Seamus Ryan and the film-reviews of Peter Connolly in the 1950s.

McGarry's own insight that no issue of legitimate concern in the Church is too sensitive to handle if the commentator is competent and the expression skilful, was only gradually formulated. And it was not the product of undiluted success. He made his mistakes. Even more significantly he suffered at times for his justified honesty and concern. New styles of communication making for a new kind of community will inevitably be experienced as threatening and resisted, sometimes to the point of retaliation. McGarry had no martyr complex and he never to my knowledge complained of unkindness he certainly experienced for some of his better but more adventurous achievements in *The Furrow*. Yet these experiences were comparatively few. His respect for persons and his concentration on issues merited widespread respect in return. The change of style did change and improve the community he wished to serve.

A further aspect of this style was his sense of fairness. He had his own priorities and preferences for the growth of the Church but they did not blind him to the necessary limitations of his own vision or to his obligation to provide space for views he did not accept. And the right to reply was properly protected. Fairness ensured balance, not the balance of fatal rigidity or of sitting on the fence or even the showy balance of the tight rope walker but the vital balance of a living and moving organism.

To change the metaphors, one's man's balanced diet may be another man's poison and balance in editing is always relative to the context and purpose of the journal. In the Irish context and in pursuit of his purpose of renewing the Irish Church pastorally, in mind and activity, McGarry interpreted his respect for his readers and his writers in a way that showed real esteem for what they cherished but recognised a potential for growth in various directions that some of them did not yet recognise. His balancing act was not only in relation to the present time and to the current readers but also to their past and their future. To give a lead and yet to keep in touch with the main body of the faithful in a searching test for any man's pastoral and editorial judgment. McGarry passed the test.

Respect for persons means respect for all persons and fundamentally equal respect for all persons. Few people had more genuine respect for Church authority, office and person, than McGarry. His one-faced approach was an expression of this. If he had criticisms to make, and he had, he made them face-to-face. If there were views he thought authority should hear, he gave them a public airing. His honesty and courage in all this did not diminish his loyalty to the Church and to its structures. They were rather an affirmation of loyalty. As he was personally no bishop-baiter, so theologically he accepted the papal and episcopal structures of the Church and worked faithfully within them. Yet his implicit principle of communication and its basically equal regard for all persons, had important implications for the full living reality of the Church as opposed to its anatomy or framework.

Lay contributors and readers were an early feature of *The*

177

Furrow and contributed to the change in style in ecclesiastical communication. Their 'outsider' status was gradually transformed into full membership of the communicating Church and so transformed the Church itself. Theologically and journalistically this reached its climax at Vatican II. In Ireland the way had been prepared by *The Furrow* and the journalists who became the immediate messengers of Vatican II and subsequent developments in the Church have all acknowledged their debt to McGarry's inspiration and guidance. Church affairs and theological debate had become proper subjects of serious, sober and objective journalism in Ireland. In communications and so as a community the Irish Church was coming of age.

Adulthood is not readily achieved and the old paternalism was not so easily banished. It retains a strong hold still. What *The Furrow* fostered and what many church leaders and committed lay-folk increasingly desired was the ease and openness of communication which is based on shared life and love and not inhibited by power and fear. Some implications of this are precisely and terrifyingly theological, in discerning God primarily as sharing life and love or as exercising power and inspiring fear. The God of threatening power and fear is the shadow-side of the God of Jesus Christ, who is the God of life and love; a shadow-side based on our failure and rejection caused by our sin. Yet where sin abounded, grace abounds even more. The power and fear are eclipsed by the forgiving, restoring and transforming gift of life and love offered to us in the person and achievement of Jesus Christ.

A fearful community, where communications are inhibited by power-play, cannot effectively preach and witness to the God of Jesus Christ. Even a protective and paternalist Church in which the fathers (and grandfathers) regard and treat as children the whole range of lay members, infants, adolescents, mature adults and the elderly, is not the community of friends to which Jesus referred in his final discourse or the People of God indicated to us in Vatican II's Constitution on the Church. Of course these are caricatures, simplifications and exaggerations of some unattractive features. In so far as they existed, *The Furrow* style of communication helped to correct them. How far they may still exist may well be revealed by examining the styles of communication in vogue

178

between bishops and priests, clergy and laity. The respect for persons, the coherence of the public and private face, the honesty, courage, fairness and sense of equality which came to characterise *The Furrow* as a means of communication and a community-shaper can never be taken for granted in any human institution, not even the Church. To invoke another caricature, Orwell's 'Newspeak' may have its ecclesiastical imitators. The temptation to it may be discerned and resisted by accepting the criteria and model provided by McGarry in editing *The Furrow*.

The Issues

If the style is the man, the issues might be said to be the situation, but not quite. A principle of selection is always at work so that the situation is interpreted in the light of the purposes of the pastoral renewal; and of the interests of the editor — which undoubtedly changed over the years.

The needs of the situation and the interest of the editor seemed to coincide neatly in two topics which received a good deal of attention through special numbers, articles, correspondence and other forms in the early years — emigration and preaching. Preaching was McGarry's professional responsibility and he gave quite a lot of attention to it in *The Furrow*, involving lay assessment and advice and providing sermon notes to help with the weekly task. Emigration might have seemed a 'natural' to a West of Ireland man. During summer holidays he had worked in a parish in London. In both cases he sought a detached picture of the actual situation with a view to providing effective help in so far as it was needed. And in both cases he caused some offence to interested parties. Yet his style prevailed and his commitment ensured more realism in discussion of the problems and application of the remedies.

These two issues typify in many ways McGarry's interests and approach. They were genuine pastoral problems. Discussion of them, mostly in private, ranged from triumphalist complacency to offensive or defensive indignation. And practically, little was done. The developed programmes for emigrant chaplains which subsequently emerged must have

been at least greatly assisted by the persistent and cool approach of *The Furrow*. How far preaching was in practice
affected may be more open to debate but certainly the provision of preachers' aids from sermon notes to communications centres and theology courses became something of a
growth industry.

Embedded in these issues was the saving mission of the
Irish Church and its effectiveness. This was the deeper basis
of *The Furrow*'s interests. The particular interests which continued to rest on this deeper basis emerged in the interaction
between the editor with his small band of helpers and the
situation of the Church in Ireland and in the world at large.
One important area of the interaction centred around
McGarry's own cultural interests. Particularly fruitful examples of this were the film and theatre reviews and the eventual
publication of a quarterly supplement on Sacred Art and
Architecture. The encouragement which this gave to younger
Irish artists and architects in the 1960s was very great and its
influence on the subsequent style of church design and decor-
ation very significant. Again there were theological implications in respecting the professionalism and faith of the artist
and in recognising that the divine dimension in all such human
achievement could only properly exist where the artist was
true to himself and his art. The lessons of the incarnation in
revealing the divine by affirming, as well as restoring and
transforming, the human inspired *The Furrow* to combine
its 'sacred' and 'profane' interests in fruitful tension.

The equally fruitful tension between the Church universal
and the Church domestic found expression in the early sur-
veys of reviews from various continents, in reports of events
and ideas from around the world, in publishing official
documentation and ultimately in commissioning or translating critical articles by key authors throughout the Catholic
Church from Cardinals Pellegrino and Suenens to Karl Rahner
and Bernard Häring.

This process was accelerated by Vatican II. In the years
of the Council the poles of the 'sacred' and the 'universal'
seemed for a time to obscure almost entirely those of the
profane and the domestic. The liturgy was given pride of
place both by personal inclination and by conciliar prefer-
ment. (It was the first Constitution officially approved and

published and had the most obvious and immediate practical implications.) McGarry's own dramatic and artistic interests as well as his work in revising the Irish Ritual, for example, peculiarly fitted and inclined him to emphasise the liturgy in the leadership and educational work of *The Furrow.* A great deal was achieved in Ireland in this area in quite a short time and without much of the confrontation or wild experimentation that surfaced elsewhere. To all this McGarry and *The Furrow* contributed notably. If in his late years, particularly after his parochial experience, he was less enthusiastic about the achievements of the liturgical reform, it was his sense of realism at work again. In spite of all the effort, serious limitations remained and McGarry was alert to the sources of some of these limitations at least. He saw the possibility of and need for a more profound personal sense of prayer than participation in the liturgy frequently provided. And he recognised the interaction between the reality or unreality of the local community as a community and its expression in the liturgy.

His growing interest in prayer and prayer-movements and in the role and influence of the Spirit naturally found its way into *The Furrow.* Hence the various series on the Life of the Spirit, the invitations to authors recognised in this field such as Simon Tugwell, Noel Dermot O'Donoghue and John Dalrymple, the reviews of the growing list of books in this area and reports on various prayer-movements and conferences. He himself participated in the movement and attended the conferences with obvious enjoyment and benefit. Yet for all his commitment to the life of prayer his personal equation together with his editorial judiciousness made him a sympathetic supporter rather than an enthusiastic convert.

The Furrow had always displayed a sensitivity about social problems. There was its early pioneering work on emigration and alcoholism, its concern for the influence and proper use of the media, its attention to marriage and family life, its outstanding contribution to relations between the Churches. It had a strong consciousness of Irish responsibility to the third world at least through the missions. The social soil in which our Gaelic roots had developed, it always took seriously. Yet the whole political dimension of life seemed for the most part to pass it by. Of course there were occasional articles

181

such as Denis Hurley's on Church-State Relations, or Donal Barrington's on the Churches' Report on Violence or Conor Cruise O'Brien's review article on *Church, State and Nation*. The Northern troubles naturally surfaced in discussions on ecumenism, violence or integrated education. The overall impression remains however that the whole socio-political field including such obvious areas as education was not thoroughly or persistently confronted. And this despite the fact that in the Church as a whole as well as in Ireland so much of Christ's saving mission depends on the interaction between Church, state and society.

It may be that to men of McGarry's generation, the achievement of independence and the tragedy of civil war somehow combined to inhibit their awareness of the tangled and sometimes destructive interaction between Church and state which developed in Ireland or the problems posed to the structures of society as well as to its goodwill by the neglected and deprived. Or perhaps he just thought that work was being adequately catered for elsewhere e.g. in *Christus Rex/Social Studies*. In any event this may subsequently appear as the greatest gap in the issues treated by *The Furrow* in his editorship. He was certainly beginning to recognise its presence himself in the last couple of years, not least because of the interaction, as I said, between liturgical community and 'secular' community, between believing community, artistic community and political community.

Conclusion

It is this interaction and challenge which Ireland frequently misses. Church and leaders too easily live within their little boxes issuing communiqués from time to time. Politicians or artists or writers or academics or business people are prone to do the same. The richness and diversity of Peadar O'Donnell and J. G. McGarry mark them out as two of the more creative Irish people of their time and as signs in turn of the profound Creator-spirit of all times.

14.

Free
to Hope

THE PASTORAL Constitution on the Church in the Modern World typifies in many ways the purpose and character of Vatican II. This council was not occasioned by any great doctrinal crisis, unlike its predecessors from Nicea to Trent. It did not propose any doctrinal decisions or definitions, unlike Vatican I. *Aggiornamento*, clearly expressing what John XXIII had in mind, and catchword of the sixties, had a pastoral ring. The 'up-dating' was to enable the Church to preach the Gospel more effectively in the modern world. The pastoral constitution, which was first mooted by Cardinal Suenens in the course of the council's work and not envisaged in the original schemata, sought to capture the essentially pastoral spirit of the council and the world-wide scope of its concerns. The *signs of the times* and the *agenda set by the modern world*, as the phrases went, were to be scrutinised by the council fathers in discerning the contemporary call of the Spirit and the contemporary significance of the Gospel.

The radical change in Church attitudes to the 'world' signalled by Vatican II may be illustrated most dramatically by contrasting the constitution of 1965 with the *Syllabus of Errors* of 1864. There are qualifications to be made, of course. The circumstances of a Church under siege from so many directions in the 1860s did not apply in the 1960s. (Yet if some of the council's preparatory documents and their sponsors — John XXIII's 'prophets of doom' — were to be taken at their face value, the siege mentality of a fortress Church (*Il Baluardo* of Cardinal Ottaviani) was still alive in Roman circles.) The adjustments to the modern world, and

183

the increasingly positive evaluation of its development, had begun in the Vatican with Leo XIII, successor to Pius IX. Despite the crisis of Modernism in the 1900s and its small-scale replay in the 'fifties, that positive evaluation of the modern world by the Churches continued to grow even in Rome, particularly in social teaching and human rights (Leo XIII, Pius XI and Pius XII), in concern for peace (Benedict XV), in biblical studies and in understanding of the role of science (Pius XII). In the world Church, as it now really was, from Asia and Africa to the Americas, new life and vigour and distinctive experience were preparing the way for a challenge to European traditions and norms. But reading the positive signs in that ambiguous century from Syllabus to Vatican II could scarcely have prepared many council fathers for the radicality and richness of what came to be known, by its first words, as the constitution *Gaudium et Spes*, 'Joy and Hope'. The very words themselves seemed an unlikely slogan to people used to the ascetic, almost grim, features of Pius XII or to the standard newspaper headlines, 'Church condemns', and 'Bishops warn'.

The change of mood was no mere ecclesiastical reflection of the 'swinging sixties', although the Church undoubtedly influenced and was influenced by the cultural, political and economic optimism of the times. For a short time, the two Johns, Pope and United States President, seemed together to symbolise the 'new frontier', new humanity in which a real liberation of humankind from fear and oppression, hunger and war, was possible. For the council fathers, mood was less significant than the slow, critical acceptance of the intellectual, political and scientific achievements of the previous two hundred years, from which the Church at the highest level had been generally insulated and to which it was frequently resistant. The values of the Enlightenment, of the liberal revolution, combined with the associated development in the physical and human sciences, were now largely accepted and critically integrated into much of the Church's life and thinking. *The Church in the Modern World* was the highlight of this development, but many other Vatican II documents, such as that on Religious Liberty, on Revelation (with the subsequent statement on the study of the Gospels), on Ecumenism and non-Christian religions, even on the Church itself, reflected much of the modern view of humanity, which had sprung from the European Enlightenment.

Gaudium et Spes, although stemming from a council which represented a world Church in a sense hitherto impossible, remained basically a European document. The strong North American influence was European in origins, tone and concern. The rest of the world Church largely echoed the European dominance which so many particular countries had shaken off politically – but not culturally, economically or religiously. The break-through achieved by the document remains of world significance because at least the particular crises tackled, political organisations and human rights, peace and war, economic power, marriage and the family are common to all. And the manner of speaking and thinking, for all its European provenance, has, for the historical reason of earlier European imperialism, relevance for very many of the cultures, countries and Churches of the rest of the world. But – and the *buts* come tumbling out – for Asians and Africans and Latin Americans, for those on the fringe of Europe like Ireland, for those on the other side of the great European divide in Poland and the other socialist countries, even for the peoples most directly concerned with the legacy of the Enlightenment in central and western Europe and North America, a balanced appreciation of such an adventurous and exciting document as *Gaudium et Spes* must also look at some of the limitations.

These will emerge, I hope, by attending to the more specific purpose of this article – a consideration of the Church as the believing people of this island of Ireland, in the Irish circumstances of the mid-eighties rather than Europe of the mid-sixties. Ireland is now, politically, economically and culturally more fully and consciously part of Europe than it was in the 1960s. Accession to the European Economic Community has focused much attention on Brussels and Strasbourg, in political and economic matters, while cultural and recreational links with other European centres have increased enormously. In other ways Ireland and Europe are more consciously integrated into the global village of the world. A reflection on the theme of 'Church in the World' will be more aware of the distinctiveness of

185

(local) Churches and (local) worlds, while also sensitive to the intimate interlinking of these Churches and of these worlds.

A Positive Adventure: the Gift and Challenge of Modernity

By seeking to integrate into a Christian perspective the positive values of two centuries of political and scientific progress, Vatican II offered a considerable challenge to believers everywhere. This was certainly true of Ireland. The relationship between Catholicism and democracy in Ireland in the early nineteenth century had been a matter of some admiration among European Catholics. And the transition in the early twentieth century from colony to stable parliamentary democracy might, in the light of the subsequent break-up of European empires, be no less worthy of admiration. In this respect no one could claim that the political legacy of the Enlightenment had no impact in Ireland. Yet it remained true that the relationship between the Catholic commitment of the great majority of the Irish people and liberal political values was never properly worked out in theory or in practice. In the decades between independence and Vatican II, various circumstances at home (economic difficulties, for example) and abroad (the rise of communism and fascism) combined to obscure the basically liberal and social thrust of Irish democratic republicanism. In the changing circumstances of the 1960s Vatican II provided the spark for many thoughtful Irish Catholics and Protestants as they sought explicit reconciliation between their Christianity (Catholic and Protestant), their Irishness and their citizenship of the modern world. The advances and regressions which Irish Christians, as Churches and as individuals, have experienced over the last twenty years reflect their further struggles in search of dynamic reconciliation between their Christian, Irish and modern strands.

The suspicion of human reason, human freedom and human progress which characterised so much of the Catholic Church's attitude over two hundred years accorded poorly with an older tradition which had defended basic human goodness against innumerable dualist and manichaean movements and had resisted the very pessimistic view of humanity espoused

186

by certain reformers. The earlier theologies which reached their climax in the work of St Thomas Aquinas, and the later ones which took their inspiration from him, should be very unhappy with the Syllabus of Errors and its associated attitudes. *Gaudium et Spes* with other documents of Vatican II finally overcame that suspicious mentality. Catholics need no longer feel guilty about being members of intellectual, cultural and political movements shaped by Enlightenment values. They could be truly 'modern', even if, like everybody else who took the Enlightenment seriously, they should not be uncritical acceptors of what passed for modernity.

Documentary regard for reason, personal freedom and social progress is no guarantee of adequate practice, in Church or state. Too many state constitutions and political prog- rammes which enthusiastically endorse these values have little effect in practice. The Proclamation of 1916, the Democratic Programme of the First Dáil, and a series of subsequent docu- ments including the 1937 Constitution, have proclaimed ideals and ambitions for the Irish people which have only been partially realised and sometimes openly abandoned. Church leaders and members are not necessarily better than politicians and citizens in implementing their own finest aspirations. Yet the openness which has characterised the Catholic Church over the past twenty years, for all the con- fusion and tensions to which it has frequently led, is a splendid achievement. Such openness has influenced the Church in Ireland, as the pages of *Doctrine and Life*, under the editorship of Austin Flannery, bear witness. The reason- able and fair-minded examination of controversial topics, the respect for the personal freedom and integrity of those who differ, the recognition that social privation and oppres- sion are of human making and require human re-making: there has been improvement in all these areas, essential as they are to the health of Irish society and to the health of the Churches in Ireland. The struggle to establish them re- ceived considerable impetus with Vatican II and the *Church in the Modern World*.

The shadows of the eighties, after the bright lights of the sixties and seventies, have underlined the fragile nature of respect for reason, freedom and social progress in many countries, including Ireland. The Churches must recognise their responsibility in protecting these essential human values in their own internal structures and conversations, and in their contribution to the wider society. It is not an unusual irony of history which finds Church leaders protecting human rights and values of which their predecessors were suspicious. The irony is multiple. Some of the greatest threats to enlightenment values have come from people who consciously espoused that tradition. Churches, which resisted the tradition and now promote many of its values, were often in their past resistant to these values, betraying some of the deepest and best strands in their own traditions. The recovery of the humanism of Thomas Aquinas, or the acceptance of humanity's 'joy and hope, grief and anguish' (paragraph 1), by *Gaudium et Spes* does not preclude further ironic twists in their attitudes and practices. The Churches, Irish and universal, have in the recent past occasionally surrendered to fear and restrictiveness out of keeping with the grand vision of Vatican II.

The challenge of modernity accepted by *Gaudium et Spes* called for a Christian believer of conviction, integration, and commitment. Conviction, far from being blind and unreasoning, develops through an honest wrestling with the real and reasonable difficulties presented by life in the world today. Difficulties which penetrate mind and heart and bones and finally disintegrate bodily life are not banished by repeating the formulae learned in childhood. Adult faith is the fruit of adult struggles. Such adult faith can be craggy and awkward for oneself and one's guides. The administrative comfort of an unquestioning Church in a world of questions can only undermine genuine Christian faith. It is the responsibility of Church leaders and ministers, whether ordained or not, to provide a context in which people's real questions may be honestly voiced and fairly explored. That mandate from Vatican II, now more urgent in Ireland, is as yet far from adequate fulfilment. Adult theology groups, developments in catechetics, more critical and intelligent religious publications, occasional radio and television programmes, all contribute to the development of faith by personal conviction among a wide range of Irish people. The search for superficial 'supernatural' phenomena does not. The task is enormous, and some of the labourers do not seem entirely convinced.

Integration, as a feature of the Christian believer, enables one to cherish every aspect of the world as God-given in creation and God-accepted in incarnation, redemption, and resurrection. Flight from this world of God involves flight from God. The celebration of the cosmos, of the gifts of creation, is central to *Gaudium et Spes*, in terms which echo de Chardin's vision of the cosmos as the divine *milieu*. And with the gifts of creation come the gifts of creativity, which God has shared with humanity, and which issue in both the humble and the masterly achievements of human culture. From the simple sentence to Dante's *Divine Comedy*, from cave scratching to Picasso's *Guernica*, from basic drum-beat to final symphony, from stone-sharpening to laser beam, the astonishing creativity of human beings has extended the beauty and power of the cosmos, has created a new world of culture and technology. The *gaudium* is multiplied as Paul Henry's Achill joins the Achill we know. The *spes* is indefinitely expanded as technical expertise heals disease and overcomes drought and desert. There is a lot of celebrating to be done, a lot of thanksgiving, of standing in awe before the Himalayas and the Parthenon, of attending to the achievement of, the mastery of, so many things in nature and in culture.

A more ancient Irish Christianity rejoiced in natural beauty and erupted in cultural achievement. The civilisation, in Kenneth Clark's terms, which the Irish monks preserved, developed and restored to Europe, was often cultivated in places of wild natural beauty like the islands of Sceilig and of Aran. The monks felt the pulse of that beauty in their own spiritual pilgrimages while in learning, language and illustration they carried on the sacred heritage of human cultural creativity.

Nineteenth-century restoration of Irish Catholicism had not the time or resources or sensibility to renew that tradition. The impoverishment was reinforced by general Church suspicion of the current trumpeting of human achievement. In regard to one of the greatest created and creative gifts, sexuality, a dualism, which was not peculiarly Catholic or Irish, exercised a very diminishing influence. The treatment of sex and marriage in *Gaudium et Spes* resumed the celebratory attitude which the Hebrew and Christian traditions had, at their best, enjoyed. The impact of this development was very noticeable in Ireland. With better preparation for couples, and a greater sense of love and life, sex and marriage could be more fully integrated as gifts of God and more deeply celebrated as human joys.

The hope, like the joy, was also in and of this world and not just displaced to the next. It connected with human and social progress, which had been such a feature of western civilisation in recent centuries. Human goodness and human ingenuity should and could harness the resources of the cosmos to overcome poverty, oppression and disease. Like Peadar O'Donnell's islanders, most people in the world die when they die because they are poor. The council voiced its hope of overcoming this poverty unto death, so that all might live in accordance with their God-given human dignity. Despite its essentially hopeful message, the council did not ignore the fact of persistent and widespread oppression and the deep-rooted obstacles to its removal. And it was well aware of the dangers to the lives of nations and peoples from war as well as from poverty and injustice. Discussion of the subject included a clear rejection of total warfare, and of those acts of war 'directed to the indiscriminate destruction of whole cities or vast areas with their inhabitants' (paragraph 80). The reappraisal of war in the light of nuclear weapons, for which the document calls, had already begun.

The hope of progress towards an international community maintaining peace between nations and ensuring respect for the right of individuals, which the council shared with the aspirations of the United Nations Charter, made better sense in 1965, perhaps, than in 1985. Yet, both the constitution and the charter are critical markers for Christians and their fellow-humans in the continuing struggle for peace and justice. They provide markers for Irish people also, whose need for peace and justice at home, and whose commitment to it abroad, have greatly intensified since the council. It may be at this point that one should move from considering the remarkable positive achievements of the constitution and their persisting validity, to the limitations which derive partly from its origins, and partly from the changed circumstances of the world in which the Church now has to function.

The Western/Northern-European dominance of the Church up to and including Vatican II did, as indicated earlier, greatly influence the agenda, the approach and the style of *Gaudium et Spes*. The distinctiveness and limitations of that European mode were quickly exposed in Latin America, as the Churches there sought to relate achievements and aspirations of the Council, and particularly the teaching on Church and world, to their condition of poverty and oppression. 'Liberation theology' and 'Church of the Poor', already widely accepted by the time of Medellín in 1968, revealed a very different agenda and approach from the liberal concerns and attitudes of Rome in 1965. Actually, *Gaudium et Spes* itself, as well as papal documents on issues of justice and peace (*Mater et magistra, Pacem in Terris* and *Populorum Progressio*) prepared the way for this more radical analysis of the Church in the world, and for the more radical response needed. The temptation to individualism, which liberal reforms frequently involve, and from which *Gaudium et Spes* did not entirely escape, becomes irrelevant in the context of the mass poverty and privation faced by the Churches in Latin America and other third world areas. The economic form of liberalism in particular, with its powerful and powerless, centre and periphery, dominant and dominated in a so-called world market economy, becomes an instrument of oppression of the powerless, the peripheral and the dominated. The west, the north, Europe — in their oppressive roles — no longer provide the Christian inspiration and theological analysis which southern/third world countries need. Theological imperialism also must come to an end. *Gaudium et Spes*, despite its great positive achievements, which have validity also among the deprived, must be supplemented and eventually transformed in these very different worlds.

Even for a country like Ireland, European but on the continent's periphery, for long politically colonised and still economically very dependent, *The Church in the Modern World* could not always read correctly the signs of the times. The Enlightenment values of respect for reason, for individual freedom and for social progress, were, however, at least as much in need of critical integration into Irish Catholic thought and life as anywhere in Europe. That integration is still incomplete if one is to judge by some of the topics and the manner of current public controversy.

The most serious limitation in the constitution applies to central as much as to peripheral Europe, as much to the dominant countries of the west as to the dominated elsewhere. In reading the signs of the times, insufficient attention was paid to the tragic dimensions of the history of Europe in the twentieth century. The fall of empires, the experience of two great fratricidal wars, the east-west division after 1945, and, above all, the chilling counter-sacrament of the Holocaust, summarise a tragic transformation of Europe in the fifty years leading up to Vatican II. As so many council fathers and most theologians (mainly European) had actually lived through so much of that tragic experience, it is all the more surprising how little explicit and existential impact it had on their deliberations and conclusions.

It could be argued that the council as a whole, and the pastoral constitution in particular, wished to offer a message of hope to the world and not engage in a depressing review of recent tragedy. This might be more urgent in view of the frequently negative reactions of the Church of Siege in the nineteenth and early twentieth centuries to the achievements and aspirations of the secular world. And the constitution did intend to deal with the grief and anguish, as well as the joy and hope, of humanity. In the immediate aftermath, the response in Church and in world confirmed the judgment of the bishops and theologians in adopting such a positive stance.

After twenty years, and still grateful for the achievement, it is important to reflect on the failure to deal more fully with the tragedy of humanity as it developed in twentieth century Europe. Theological and ecclesiastical discussion of tragedy and evil can sometimes be self-righteous in its attitude, trivialising in its analysis, and banal in its prescriptions. The recent tragedy of Europe was a tragedy of Christians, of the Church. Christian believers and leaders were directly implicated in the fratricidal wars. The genocidal programme which issued in the Holocaust had deep and tangled anti-Semitic roots among Christians, and could only develop so successfully because too few had the insights and courage to resist.

Until European Christians are able to confront their failure

192

and recognise the tragedy and evil of this century, their expressions of solidarity with the sufferings and hopes of the rest of humanity will remain rather superficial. Here lies the most serious theological flaw in *Gaudium et Spes*. Hope does not evade failure, tragedy, evil. In the Christian pilgrimage hope arises through and beyond failure. For St Paul, 'suffering produces endurance, endurance produces character, and character produces hope' (Rom. 5:3-4). Endurance, confronting and wrestling with the suffering, precede hope. Paul's hope is based on the death and resurrection of the Lord. Death, with its darkness and destruction, must be fully accepted by Jesus before his acceptance by the Father in resurrection. The cries of need and near-despair in Gethsemane and on Calvary expose the tragic depths of human destruction and human abandonment. The acknowledgement of all that is a necessary prelude to the gift of hope.

The tragedy of Europe could be the beginning of truly Christian hope. But first, Christians must accept their own failure, their own responsibility, their own contribution to the imperialism, self-righteousness and destructiveness which characterised so much recent European history. The Holocaust and anti-Semitism are particular signs of the times for Christians. Yet even the admirable attempt, in the council's document on non-Christian religions, *Nostra Aetate*, to move away from the traditional Christian treatment of the Jews does not properly face the Holocaust or Christian involvement in it. To acknowledge the tragedy and our complicity in it, is essential to the hope embodied in Christian conversion.

Ireland has had its own share of fratricidal killing and of Christian involvement in the tragedy. The last sixteen years in particular have exposed the violence between brothers, both Irish and both Christian. So far, as a people and as Churches, we seem unable to acknowledge the destructiveness which is in us, and which is fuelled by some deadly combination of our political, racial and religious allegiances. The Irish Churches in the Irish world may not take into themselves the motto *Gaudium et Spes* until they first acknowledge their role in maintaining the *luctus et angor* 'the grief and anguish' of the people of our time (par. 1). That grief and that anguish extend in Ireland to a wide range of people, handicapped and deprived in a variety of ways. To convey hope of relief, liberation, fulfilment, in Christ's name, to the mentally and physically handicapped, to the chronically and terminally ill, to the homeless, to the Travellers, to the unemployed, to prisoners, to homosexuals, to all the other deprived minorities, to women in their more general frustrations and privations, is a daunting set of tasks. Without sharing the suffering, acknowledging complicity, and working for change, Christians have no right to speak of hope. This may be more deeply true of the 'national question' where Church affiliation has always been a contributory factor. When Irish Christians finally and fully acknowledge that, we may hope to hope.

Dóchas Linn? Are We Free to Hope?

For the world that is Ireland now, the Catholic Church has much to cherish and develop from the Constitution *Gaudium et Spes*. A Church which understands itself as at the service of the Kingdom of God, proclaimed and inaugurated by Jesus Christ, will be on the alert to discern and promote the Kingdom values of truth and freedom, justice and peace. It is not easy for the Church as people or hierarchy to remember its servant status. There is a natural self-inflation of Church and Church-leaders which permits human persons and institutions to obscure and even replace the reign or kingship of God. A parallel, more frequent, and more far-reaching self-inflation by State and politician, forgetful in turn of *their* serving role, leads to Church-state confrontations and sacred-secular power struggles, absorbing energies which should be spent, at least for the Church, in loving service.

Resistance by the Church to activities of the state may well be required in fidelity to its mission. So, for that matter, may resistance by statesmen to certain activities of churchmen. Tension and conflict can never simply be wished away. Yet the Church's mission to transcend the power-structures and the power-struggles of the princes of this world by loving and liberating service on the model of Jesus should make Church leaders sensitive to the temptations of power within the Church itself and in the wider society. This applies with particular force to the Irish Churches, Catholic and Protestant, south and north. In their internal treatment of their own

194

members they convey to many people a sense of difficulty with the *different* that may easily become intolerance. James Good and David Armstrong may have received exceptional treatment but they are limit cases of a pressure which many others have experienced. In the broader society, the restrictive and repressive roles of the Churches appear more significant to many people, not all of them enemies.

Without confusing liberty with trivalising permissiveness, the Churches might well concentrate their efforts, for a year at least, on translating and promoting, in Irish ecclesial and political terms, the great Pauline theme of 'the freedom of the Christian'. If the Churches, in their separateness and together, took a year out to explore, preach, and actively implement the multiple dimensions of freedom, human and Christian, they would render signal service to Gospel and culture, to Kingdom and society. Ireland and the Irish Churches would have much to record in terms of both joy and hope.

Ireland as tragedy should provide a constant counter to the promethean tendencies of unexamined liberalism or progressivism. With our sense of history and experience of failure we should be able to supply the tragic dimension missing from *Gaudium et Spes*. A sense of tragedy may also be self-indulgent and self-inflating. It has been so too often in Ireland. Drowning in our sorrows, we have sometimes become exhibitionists and escapists who refuse to confront, or attempt to overcome, our own real self-made problems. Recognising the tragic side of life is not, in Christian faith, an excuse for evading life but an opportunity for enduring through suffering, hoping through endurance, and so entering into transformation. The fatalism of 'It will be all the same in a hundred years' may swing to a trivial consumerist 'Eat, drink and be merry', without any serious effort to combine the sense of life as adventurous call with a sense of the tragic. Where *Gaudium*, genuine rejoicing in life, is maintained in creative interchange with 'the notion of some infinitely gentle, infinitely suffering thing', the *Spes*, Christian *hope*, that goes through and beyond Calvary in resurrection, is an authentic possibility.